CANNABIS MEDICINE
A Guide to the Practice of Cannabinoid Medicine

David Bearman, M.D.
with Maria Pettinato, PhD, RN

Edited by Angela Bacca

Copyright © 2018 by David Bearman

ISBN 9781690856962

First Edition

10 9 8 7 6 5 4 3 2 1

Cover Design by Cathy Feldman

To order this book in quantity please contact:
Dr. David Bearman's Mecial Practice
dbearman420@gmail.com • 805-961-9988

Printed in United States of America

FOREWORD

This new *Cannabis Medicine: A Guide to the Practice of Cannabinoid Medicine* is meant as a quick introduction and overview of cannabis, cannabinoids, and the endocannabinoid system (ECS) for both health care professionals and discerning patients. The material herein provides a foundation for a beginning appreciation of the medicinal value of cannabis and cannabinoids and their mechanism of action. It is a primer designed to provide an introduction to the science of cannabis. It contains helpful clinical and educational information meant to aid those considering the use of medicinal cannabis and/or the practice of cannabinoid medicine.

This short book provides a framework for understanding what the deluge of cannabis and cannabinoid research and clinical experiences are revealing about cannabis use in medical practice. The information it contains opens the door to a more nuanced understanding of the endo-cannabinoid system and the clinical applications of cannabis and cannabinoids.

ACKNOWLEDGEMENTS

Cannabis is an over 4,000-year-old medicine that was in the American medical mainstream for over 70 years. It was in the United States Pharmacopeia from 1850-1942. Now we are seeing cannabis's reintroduction back into mainstream medicine. This gradual, grudging recognition and acceptance of the safety and medical utility of cannabis by contemporary health care professionals stands on the shoulders of many.

The production of this resource owes much to too many people to mention them all. I appreciate the important contributions of my collaborator Maria Pettinato, RN, PhD, my publisher Cathy Feldman, my editor Angela Bacca, and typists Donna O'Toole, Elizabeth Schmidt, Julie Johnson, and Christina Spencer Perry. Thanks to Jake Felice, ND and Anne Morgan, M.D., who read and commented on early drafts and to research assistant Tori Catherwood. Thanks to my wife, Lily and children, Samantha and Benjamin, for their love and support.

Recognizing Some of the Pioneers Past and Present

We stand on the shoulders of heroes whose research, insight, practical experience and moral courage have gotten us to this point. Some of these clinicians and researchers are our contemporaries and others came long before us. Here are just a few of those to whom we owe a great deal for reaching the point of some legal access to this remarkable plant and the possibility for more quality research.

The panoply of heroes includes researchers, patients and drug reformers. A few notables worth recognizing are Sir

William Osler, M.D.; William Woodward, M.D.; Morris Fishbein, M.D.; Col. James Phalen, M.D.; Raphael Mechoulam, PhD; Todd Mikuriya, M.D.; Mark Ware, M.D.; Ethan Russo, M.D.; the late California state senator John Vasconcellos (D-San Jose); Roger Pertwee, PhD; Geoffrey Guy, M.D.; Franjo Grotenhermen, M.D.; Christina Sanchez, PhD; Manuel Guzman, PhD; Melanie Dreher, RN, PhD; Jeff Hergenrather, M.D.; Martin Lee, Frank Lucido, M.D.; Fred Gardner; Lester Grinspoon, M.D.; Anne V. Morgan,M.D.; John Morgan, M.D.; Lynn Zimmer, PhD; Mary Lynn Mathre, RN; Vincenzo Di Marzo, PhD; Dustin Sulak, DO; Robert Melamede, PhD; Deborah Malha, PhD; Michelle Sexton, ND; the Board of the American Academy of Cannabinoid Medicine: Greg Carter, M.D., Arnold Leff, M.D., Chris Fichtner, M.D., David Ostrow, M.D., Arnie Morgan, M.D., and Christine Paoletti, M.D.; Representative Dana Rohrabacher (R-CA); Ethan Nadleman, PhD; Robert Randall and Irvin Rosenfeld, Independent New Drug Program participants.

TABLE OF CONTENTS

FOREWORD iii
ACKNOWLEDGEMENTS iv
Chapter 1: History 3
Chapter 2: How Does Cannabis Work in Humans? 10
Chapter 3: Dopamine and Retrograde Inhibition 17
Chapter 4: Mitochondria. 19
Chapter 5: The Human Brain 23
Chapter 6: Homeostasis 25
Chapter 7: Constituents and Chemical Characteristics 26
Chapter 8: Terpenes 35
Chapter 9: Dosing 40
Chapter 10: Routes of Administration 53
Chapter 11: Metabolism 62
Chapter 12: Medicinal Uses of Cannabis 64
Chapter 13: Side Effects of Cannabis 79
Chapter 14: Pregnancy 89
Chapter 15: Cannabis Dependence. 94
Chapter 16: Driving. 101
Chapter 17: Toxicology 105
Chapter 18: Clinical Standards 107
Chapter 19: What About the Future 114
Appendix A: Cannabis Plants 119
Appendix B: Resources on Cannabinoids 123
Glossary: Cannabis Lexicon 125
About the Authors 139
Index 141

CANNABIS MEDICINE

CHAPTER 1

History

The cannabis plant first arrived on the scene approximately 35 million years ago. *Cannabis sativa L.* is among the oldest agricultural crops in the world, cultivated for at least 10,000 years. It has been used as a food, a nutraceutical, entheogen, herbal medicine, prescription medicine and social lubricant for all of recorded human history. As Michael Pollan describes in *The Botany of Desire* (2001) the plant evolved and survived by creating cannabinoids and terpenes as a method of self-defense, both are essential to its medicinal effects in humans.

Humans have bred the cannabis plant for various uses. "Hemp" varieties of the plant are cultivated for their fiber and seeds, making hemp paper, textiles, oils and foods. "Marijuana" varieties were bred for the sticky resin produced by their flowers.

Both hemp and marijuana varieties of cannabis produce resin glands. The U.S. government established a threshold 0.3% $\triangle$-9-tetrahydrocannabinol (THC) to distinguish between cannabis plants considered "hemp" and those considered "marijuana." This distinction is completely arbitrary and has no basis in actual botanical science.[1] The use of hemp for fiber dates back at least 8,000 years.[2]

Cannabis for Pain Relief

Pain is the most common symptom that drives patients to see a physician. Cannabis has long been used as an analgesic, or painkiller. Its analgesic properties are noted in most, if not all,

---

[1] Richard E Schultes. Random thoughts and queries on the botany of cannabis. J. & A. Churchill., 1970. p. 23, 27.
[2] Zatta, Alessandro, Andrea Monti, and Gianpietro Venturi. "Eighty Years of Studies on Industrial Hemp in the Po Valley (1930--2010)." Journal of natural fibers 9, no. 3 (2012):

Cannabis Time Line

Date	Country	Event
2737 B.C.E	China	Listed in Shen Nung's pharmacopoeia
2000 B.C.E.	Egypt	Made as a drink in ancient Thebes
1000 B.C.E.	India	Used as an herbal medicine
500 B.C.E.	Persia	A principle sacrament of the Zoroastrians
450 B.C.E.	Scythia	Inhaled as an intoxicating incense
200 B.C.E.	Israel	Used as a medicine by the Essenes
700 C.E.	Middle East	Brought divine revelation to Sufi priests
c. 1200	Europe	Banned as a medicine by the Spanish Inquisition
c. 1480	Italy	Criminalized by Pope Innocent VIII
1802	France	Napoleon's soldiers return from Egypt with cannabis
1835	France	Club des Hashishines established.
1839	India	Dr. William O'Shaughnessy introduces cannabis to England
1892	U.S./Britain	Sir William Osler recommends cannabis for migraines in his textbook
1895	Britain	The Indian Hemp Drug Commission Report
1914	U.S.	Cannabis successfully excluded from Harrison Narcotics Tax Act
1931	Panama	Canal Zone, Siler Report
1937	U.S.	American Medical Association (AMA) testifies against the Marijuana Tax Act
1937	U.S.	Harry Anslinger testifies marijuana causes aggression and rage
1942	U.S.	Dr. Morris Fishbein, editor of *JAMA*, says cannabis best treatment for migraines
1943	U.S.	*Military Surgeon* publishes "The Marijuana Bugaboo" editorial
1948	U.S.	Anslinger testifies cannabis makes users passive
1949	U.S.	First modern study on the medicinal benefits of cannabis (for epilepsy)
1968	Britain	Wootton Commission Report
1969	U.S.	U.S. Supreme Court finds Marijuana Tax Act unconstitutional

Date	Country	Event
1970	U.S.	Controlled Substances Act passed
1971	U.S.	Nixon Marijuana Commission Report
1978	U.S.	Compassionate Investigational New Drug (IND) program starts
1982	U.S.	First Institute of Medicine (IOM) Report
1991	U.S.	Compassionate IND program ends
1996	U.S.	California legalizes medicinal cannabis
1997	Britain	Report of House of Lords Science & Technology Committee
1999	Britain	GW Pharmaceuticals begins research on tincture of cannabis, (nabixamols) i
1999	U.S.	California state legislature allocates $9 million for research on medical utility of cannabis
2000	U.S.	California Marijuana Research Center opens at the UCSD School of Medicine
2005	Canada	Sativex (tincture of cannabis) approved for sale by Health Canada
2007	U.S.-	DEA Office of Administrative Law judge rules in favor of Dr. Lyle Craker growing marijuana for research
2009	U.S.	Ogden Memo: Attorney General Eric Holder suspends federal raids on legal dispensaries
2010	Britain/E.U.	Sativex approved in Britain
2011	U.S.	UCSD School of Medicine releases 10-year California Marijuana Research Center report
2012	U.S.	Colorado and Washington legalize cannabis
2014-2016	U.S.	All but five states legalize some form of medical cannabis. Eight states and D.C. legalize receational cannabis
2017	U.S.	National Academy of Sciences Report: Cannabis is useful as medicine

Note: A more detailed version of this timeline is available in *Drugs Are NOT The Devil's Tools: The History of Drugs: Discrimination, Greed, the War on Drugs, and Why Medical Marijuana is Creating a New Paradigm.*

materias medica ever written. Shen Nung's Pen Ts'ao Ching (*Divine Husbandman's Classic of Materia Medica*) was the earliest Chinese pharmacopoeia. Nung is considered the Chinese God of agriculture and possibly the mythical Second Emperor of China. The Pen Ts'ao Ching was passed on by oral traditions. That tradition places its establishment in 2637 B.C.E. or 2737 B.C.E.[3]

Researchers date the oldest written compilation that still survives documenting these Chinese oral medical traditions to between 300 B.C.E. and 200 B.C.E. The original text, allegedly written in the third millennium B.C.E., no longer exists but is said to have been composed of three volumes containing 365 entries describing hundreds of medicants. The first known written record about herbal medicine was compiled between 1065 and 771 B.C.E.

Over time, the medicinal use of cannabis spread from China, India and the Middle East to Europe. Hemp was well known in Europe in the Middle Ages. It was used to make beer and as an ingredient in gruel, a common grain breakfast cereal of the time. In the 15th century, the Pope labeled cannabis as an instrument of the devil because of its healing capabilities. This papal action practically eliminated the medical use of cannabis by mainstream physicians in Europe. It was, however, used by midwives, aka witches. It may have been as late as the early 19th century that the medicinal use of cannabis was reintroduced into Europe by Dr. W.B. O'Shaughnessy, a British physician.[4]

In the late 1830s, O'Shaughnessy returned to England from India, where he was involved in putting the telegraph across the country. Upon his return, he reintroduced cannabis to Western medicine. One of the therapeutic attributes he

---

[3] Medical Cannabis A Short Graphical History China." Antique Cannabis Book. Accessed February 1, 2018. http://antiquecannabisbook.com/chap2B/China/China.htm/.

[4] O'Shaughnessy, William Brooke. "On the preparations of the Indian Hemp, or Gunjah: Cannabis indica their effects on the animal system in health, and their utility in the treatment of tetanus and other convulsive diseases." *Provincial Medical Journal and Retrospect of the Medical Sciences* 5, no. 123 (1843): 363.

discussed was cannabis's analgesic properties. Soon, by the middle of the 19th century, cannabis became an important medicine in America. It caught on quickly and was widely used in many 19th century pain relief preparations. Cannabis was prescribed in the 1890s to Queen Victoria of England by her royal physician, Sir J. Russell Reynolds, for relief of the pain of her menstrual cramps.[5]

Cannabis has been known for centuries as one of the best treatments for relief of the symptoms of migraine headaches, particularly for relief from the accompanying pain and nausea. Sir William Osler, usually acknowledged as the founder of modern medicine and one of the four founders of the John Hopkins School of Medicine, dubbed cannabis the best migraine treatment in *The Principles and Practice of Medicine* (1892), often considered the first textbook of internal medicine.

From the 1850s to the early 1940s, cannabis was a popular ingredient in both patent and prescription medications. Medicinal cannabis products were manufactured by such well known pharmaceutical firms as Eli Lilly, Squibb, Merck, Parke-Davis, Sharp and Dohme, and the Smith Brothers. In the 1920s American physicians wrote three million cannabis-containing prescriptions per year. According to the American Medical Association (AMA), in the late 1930s, the use of medicinal cannabis had decreased because the product was hard to standardize and had a relatively short shelf life.[6] It remained in the United States Pharmacopeia (USP) until 1942.[7]

---

[5] "History of Marijuana as Medicine - 2900 BC To Present," *ProCon*. Accessed February 1, 2018. https://medicalmarijuana.procon.org/view.timeline.php?timelineID=000026/.
[6] Herer, Jack, Jeff Meyers, and Leslie Cabarga. . "Cannabis Drug Use in 19th Century America," in *The emperor wears no clothes*. Ah Ha Pub., 1998. Last modified: February 1 2018. http://jackherer.com/emperor-3/
[7] Pharmacopeia, United States. "12th rev." Accessed February 1, 2018. http://antiquecannabisbook.com/Appendix/USP1942.htm/.

American Medical Association Testifies Against the Marihuana Tax Act of 1937

In 1937 Dr. William C. Woodward, a physician, attorney, chief legal counsel of the American Medical Association (AMA) and past president of the American Public Health Association (1914), testified before the House Ways and Means Committee against the Marihuana Tax Act. Dr. Woodward testified that the AMA knew of "no danger from the medicinal use of cannabis."[8]

Dr. Woodward further testified that he had contacted several agencies in the U.S. government including the United States Public Health Service, Bureau of Prisons and Children's Bureau and found they had no evidence to back up the claims being made by the first head of the Bureau of Narcotics and Dangerous Drugs (BNDD), Harry Anslinger. The BNDD would evolve over the years into the modern-day Drug Enforcement Administration (DEA).[9] Dr. Woodward said Anslinger had no evidence-based facts, all he had was a fistful of newspaper clippings. Ignoring Woodward's testimony, the Marihuana Tax Act was passed by Congress.

---

[8] Woodward, William C interviewed by The House of Representatives Committee on Ways and Means "Taxation of Marihuana." May 4, 1937. Accessed February 1, 2018. http://www.druglibrary.org/Schaffer/hemp/taxact/woodward.htm/.
[9] Ibid.

1986-1988 DEA Rescheduling Hearing

Many others have followed Dr. Woodward's 1937 lead in pointing out the incredibly low side effect profile of cannabis. In 1988, after a two-year rescheduling hearing, the DEA Chief Administrative Law Judge, Francis Young, recommended rescheduling cannabis to Schedule II. Judge Young's "Finding of Fact" stated that cannabis, or marijuana as he referred to it, was one of the safest therapeutic agents known to mankind.[10] He stated that it was safer than eating ten potatoes. This recommendation by Judge Young was rejected by George H.W. Bush's DEA Director, John Lawn.

---

[10] Drug Enforcement Administration. Young, Francis L. "In the Matter of Marijuana Rescheduling Petition - Opinion and Recommended Ruling, Findings of Fact, Conclusions of Law and Decision of Administrative Law Judge"September 6, 1988.

CHAPTER 2
HOW DOES CANNABIS WORK IN HUMANS?

The Endocannabinoid System (ECS)

The endocannabinoid system (ECS) is the largest neurotransmitter system in the human brain (Note: some argue that the Gamma-aminobutyric acid (GABA) system is bigger). Endogenous cannabinoid receptors are found in all mammalian brains and are located throughout the central and peripheral nervous systems. They are named CB-1 and CB-2.

CB1 receptors are situated in the midbrain, hippocampus, the cerebral cortex and the amygdala (which may account for the lower level of aggression in cannabis smokers). CB1 receptors are found not only in nervous tissue, as originally thought, but are also in numerous other tissue types including skin and muscle. The CB2 receptors are largely found in cells of the immune system, but they too are found in other tissues including the brain and GI tract. Few or no CB1 receptors are found in the brain stem, which is why no one has ever died as a direct result of a cannabis overdose.

The ECS is composed of ligands (molecules), ligand receptors, ligand transporters, and degrading enzymes. The ECS includes at least two neuromodulatory lipid neurotransmitters (ligands), 2AG and anandamide, two degrading enzymes (FAAH and MYGL), and at least two cannabinoid receptors that bind to the CB1 and CB2 receptors. Anandamide receptors (CB1 receptors) are also THC receptors.

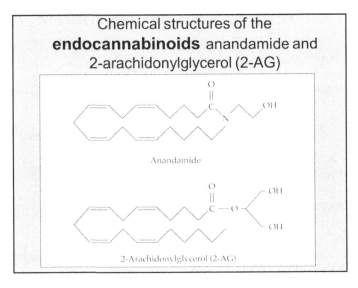

Chemical structures of the **endocannabinoids** anandamide and 2-arachidonylglycerol (2-AG)

A search of Medline reveals that since 1995 at least 25,000 articles on cannabis, cannabinoids and the ECS have been published in peer reviewed medical journals. Due to growing research interest in the ECS we are increasing our knowledge of this system on an almost daily basis, but there is still much to learn.

Principle Endocannabinoid System Components

Two principle endocannabinoid receptors
CB-1, CB-2

Other receptors
TRPR1
GPR, 18, 55, 119
PPARS

Two Enzymes that metabolize cannabinoids
FAAH (fatty acid amide hydrolase)
MAGL (monoacylglycerol lipase)

Two Endocannabinoid Neurotransmitters (aka as endogenous ligands)
Anandamide aka Arachidonoyl ethanolamine (AEA)
2 - arachidonoylglycerol (2 AG)

Two Enzymes that metabolize cannabinoids
Dopamine
Dopamine Transporter

THE ENDOCANNABINOID SYSTEM

BRAIN & NERVOUS SYSTEM
Modulates speed of neurotransmission
via Retrograde Inhibition
Critical for homeostasis
↓ Gastrointestinal mobility via the Vagus

NOSE
↑ Odor sensitivity
↑ Food-seeking behavior

MOUTH/ORAL CAVITY
↑ Neural responses to sweet taste
Regulation of taste sensitivity?

GASTROINTESTINAL TRACT
↑ Fat preference and intake
Affects speed of peristalsis

PANCREAS
↑ Insulin secretion
↑ Apoptopic activity and cancer cell death
by increasing cancer cell ceramide

LIVER
↑ Lipogenesis
↓ Insulin clearance

SKELETAL MUSCLE
↓ Insulin-dependent glucose uptake
↓ Inflammation

ADIPOSE TISSUE
↑ Adipogenesis
↑ Glucose uptake
↓ Fatty acid oxidation
↓ Mitochondrial biogenesis
Repository for THC

The endocannabinoid system "is perhaps the most important physiologic system involved in establishing and maintaining human health..."[11] The ECS is involved in a variety of physiological processes including appetite control, analgesia (pain-mediation), mood, memory, and homeostasis. "Cannabinoids are involved in the fundamental life, death and differentiation alternatives of cells...Cannabinoid receptors are present throughout the body, embedded in cell membranes..."[12] In layperson's terms you might say the human organism is extremely cannabinoid friendly, both to endogenous and exogenous (originating outside the organism) cannabinoids.

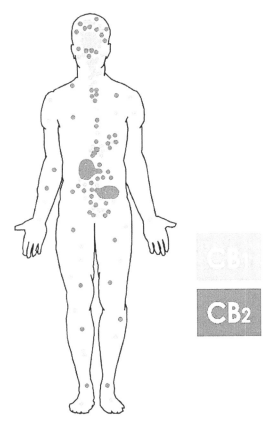

"THE ENDOCANNABINOID SYSTEM." SENSI PHARMA WEBSITE. HTTP://SENSIPHARMA.COM/ECS/

[11] Sulak, Dustin. "Introduction to the Endocannabinoid System." NORML. http://norml.org/library/item/introduction-to-the-endocannabinoid-system/.
[12] Ibid.

Non-cannabinoid receptors

There are also important non-cannabinoid receptors (receptors other than CB1 and CB2). For instance, cannabidiol (CBD) does not directly activate mitochondrial CB1 receptors. Instead, CBD binds to different receptors, including the sodium-calcium exchanger (NCX), found on the mitochondria's surface. Binding to NCX opens an ion channel to CB2 receptors, which in turn activates these receptors.

CBD plays a role in regulating intracellular calcium levels. Different levels of calcium ions have different effects. In conditions of low cellular stress, characterized by low intracellular calcium surrounding the mitochondria, CBD will increase stress by allowing calcium to flow out of the mitochondria. In high stress conditions, characterized by high levels of intracellular calcium, CBD will do the exact opposite, allowing the flow of calcium from outside to inside the mitochondria (where calcium is stored) by opening the NCX. This bidirectional calcium flow is regulated by NCX and it is one of the mechanisms whereby CBD facilitates cellular homeostasis and neuroprotection.

Cannabinoids Effect on Endocannabinoid Receptors

Receptor Binding: Orthosteric v. Allosteric

The △-9 THC molecule fits into the body's CB1 receptors like a key in a lock. This type of receptor binding is called orthosteric binding. In their article on orthosteric and allosteric binding, Martin Lee and Jahan Marcu, Ph.D, point out that CBD only partially fits into the CB1 receptor. This fit of the CBD molecules into the CB1 receptor is called "allosteric binding". By this allosteric binding, CBD thus alters the way that THC fits in the CB1 receptor.[13]

CBD decreases THC mediated euphoria by altering the way THC fits into the CB1 receptor. CBD also has many

---

[13] "Is CBD Really Non-Psychoactive?" Project CBD. Accessed February 1, 2018. https://www.projectCBD.org/science/cannabis-pharmacology/cbd-really-non-psychoactive/.

Cannabinoid Common Effects	
THC	**CBD**
Anti-Nauseant	Decreases Euphoria from THC
Appetite Stimulant	Decreased Anxiety
Anti-Depressant	Anti-Inflammatory
Relaxation	Anti-Epileptic
Analgesic	
Anti-Epileptic	

therapeutic effects including appetite stimulation, mood elevation, pain-sensation reduction, analgesic and anti-inflammation, as well as mediation of the euphorigenic effects of cannabis. According to Dr. Deborah Malka, MD, PhD and herbalist, when the dose of CBD exceeds the dose of THC in a medicinal cannabis product, CBD not only can interfere with the euphoric effect of THC but also can decrease the analgesic effect of cannabis.

Endocannabinoid Deficiency Syndrome

Daniele Piomelli, Ph.D., pharmacology professor at the University of California at Irvine (UCI), postulates that many of those suffering from attention deficit disorder (ADD), bipolar disorder, panic attacks and Tourette's Syndrome are likely to have an endocannabinoid deficiency.[14] Interestingly, these are all conditions that are related to excessive speed and frequency of neurotransmission.

Retrograde Inhibition

The ECS is critical for neuromodulation (regulating the speed of neurotransmissions) and homeostasis (regulating bodily

[14] Beltramo, Massimiliano, Fernando Rodriguez de Fonseca, Miguel Navarro, Antonio Calignano, Miguel Angel Gorriti, Gerasimos Grammatikopoulos, Adolfo G. Sadile, Andrea Giuffrida, and Daniele Piomelli. "Reversal of dopamine D2 receptor responses by an anandamide transport inhibitor." *Journal of Neuroscience* 20, no. 9 (2000): 3401-3407.

systems). This neuromodulation works on nerves by a mechanism called retrograde inhibition. Nerves communicate with each other by sending chemically mediated electrical signals across synapses (a gap between neurons). The ECS represents a mechanism by which neurons can communicate backwards (retrograde) across synapses to modulate the speed of neurotransmission.

By adding more exogenous cannabinoids, (as from cannabis, nabiximols, or dronabinol), the speed of neurotransmission is slowed through retrograde inhibition. This may be why cannabis is useful in treating such diverse medical conditions as migraine headaches, seizure disorder, ulcerative colitis, ADD/ADHD and impulse control issues, all of which appear to be related to very rapidly moving neural impulses.

CHAPTER 3
DOPAMINE'S ROLE IN RETROGRADE INHIBITION

The neuromodulators, dopamine and dopamine transporter, play an important role in the functioning of the ECS. The cannabinoid receptors are co-localized with dopamine receptors, suggesting that cannabinoids affect the release of dopamine and the dopaminergic processes. The release of dopamine slows down the speed of neurotransmission by depolarizing the presynaptic neuron. This depolarization makes it harder for the next neural impulse to stimulate the affected neuron.

This retrograde inhibition is caused by cannabinoids triggering dopamine release, which in turn increases neuronal depolarization. This mechanism of action helps prevent the brain from being inundated and overwhelmed by excessive internal and external stimuli.[15] For example, when someone has a seizure disorder, reducing the speed of neural transmission may reduce both the intensity and frequency of seizures.

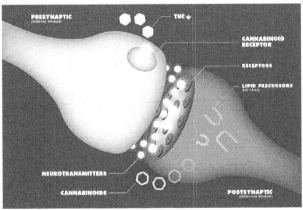

DAVID BIENENSTOCK. "HOW (AND WHY) YOUR BRAIN MAKES ITS OWN CANNABINOIDS." VICE.

[15] Miller, A. M., and N. Stella. "CB2 receptor-mediated migration of immune cells: It can go either way." *British Journal of Pharmacology* 153, no. 2 (2008): 299-308.

Dopamine

There is more than one theory on the role dopamine plays in the human brain. The following is my interpretation of existing evidence-based research.

Since cannabinoid receptors are co-localized with dopamine receptors, it is likely that cannabinoids affect the release of dopamine. It is postulated that the release of dopamine affects the intra- and extra-cellular electrolyte concentrations of effected neurons. This release of dopamine can be triggered by the presence of either exogenous or endogenous cannabinoids, depolarizes the presynaptic neuron, thereby making it harder for the following neural impulse to stimulate the neuron until it repolarizes. Releasing more dopamine, this slows the neurotransmission to the higher centers of cognition helping to process neuronal inputs of all types (e.g. sounds, colors, thoughts, and concepts).

The increased presence of cannabinoids also helps patients to focus more easily, which is clinically relevant in the treatment of conditions such as ADD and ADHD. In addition, this slowing of neurotransmission is beneficial in the case of other conditions including PTSD, Crohn's Disease, migraines, and seizure disorders.[16]

---

[16] Bienenstock, David, "How (and Why) Your Brain Makes its Own Cannabinoids," Vice. February 29, 2016. Accessed February 1, 2018.
https://www.vice.com/en_us/article/bnp4bv/how-and-why-your-brain-makes-its-own-cannabinoids/.

CHAPTER 4
MITOCHONDRIA

What are mitochondria?

Mitochondria are one of the intracellular organelles. They exist within the cells of every multicellular organism, including humans. All human cells contain mitochondria, with the exception of red blood cells. One of the main functions of mitochondria is to take high-energy molecules - such as sugars and amino acids - and convert them into adenosine triphosphate (ATP), a form of energy that the cell can use.

Symbiosis

"Originally, mitochondria were not an organelle but was itself separate from other cells," writes Martin Lee of Project CBD, author of *Smoke Signals: A Social History of Marijuana- Medical, Recreational and Scientific* (2012). Lee postulates that in the neighborhood of one-and-a-half to two billion years ago, "a cell engulfed an evolutionary precursor to a mitochondrion. But instead of digesting the mitochondrion, the two living entities formed a symbiotic relationship. The host cell would provide nutrients and a safe place for the mitochondrion to exist, and the mitochondrion would perform the [oxidative] process of cellular respiration, giving the host a more useable form of energy." This symbiotic relationship had an important impact on the emergence of multicellular organisms.[17]

Cannabinoids: Role in Mitochondria

There are three major ways that exogenous (plant based) and endogenous (produced inside the nervous system of all mammals) cannabinoids can directly modulate mitochondrial

[17] Project CBD: Mitochondria Mysteries." Project CBD. Accessed February 1, 2018. http://www.projectcbd.org/cannabinoids-and-mitochondria/.

function: activating CB1 receptors on the mitochondria, affecting the mitochondrial membrane and binding to other (non-cannabinoid) receptors on the mitochondria's surface.

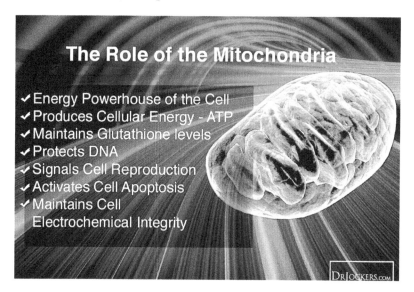

Mitochondrial CB1 receptors

Cannabinoid receptors are found on cell membranes. They are the most prevalent G-coupled protein receptors (GCPR) in the human brain and central nervous system and are the most popular cellular target for pharmaceutical treatment. An estimated 15 percent of all the CB1 receptors exist on the mitochondrial cell membrane. In muscle tissue containing CB1 receptors, half of these receptors are localized on the mitochondria.

Mitochondrial CB1 receptors are not structurally distinct from the CB1 receptors that are on the cell's outer surface, but their effects are quite different. Research associate and science writer Adrian Devitt-Lee provides a useful analogy to explain this difference: "Light switches may look the same from room to room, but they are connected to different circuitry throughout the house, and so turning the switch on or off in different places causes different outcomes."[18]

---

[18] Ibid.

Mitochondrial Cannabinoids May Help Explain Some Contradictions

Cannabinoid research findings appear to be riddled with contradictions. This is because cannabinoids frequently exert opposite effects in different situations. How are CBD and THC able to balance physiological excess as well as deficiency? Why does a small dose of cannabis stimulate while a large dose tends to sedate? Why does a low therapeutic does act as an anti-nauseant while a higher recreational dose is sometimes associated with hyperemesis? How is it possible that cannabinoid compounds can destroy cancer cells while leaving healthy cells unscathed? Modern research is working at uncovering the answers to these and many other questions.

Mitochondria Structural Features

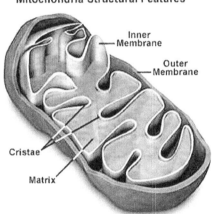

Examining the role of mitochondria sheds some light on the perplexing and confounding aspects of the endocannabinoid system. Cannabinoid activity in the mitochondria is complicated. In low-stress conditions, cannabinoids often increase mitochondrial activity and cellular respiration, triggering a process called autophagic cellular repair. Cannabinoids can also buffer high-stress conditions and protect cells by decreasing mitochondrial activity. We may improve our understanding of the role of endocannabinoids by looking at mitochondria more closely and some of that research is currently ongoing.

Free Radicals & Phytocannabinoids

The human body requires energy. It gets it in the form of Adenosine Triphosphate (ATP) that is made in the mitochondria. Creating this energy produces free radicals that can cause cell damage. Antioxidants such as THC and CBD reduce these effects by mopping up the free radicals. This is one of the attributes of the cannabis plant that is thought to contribute to its anti-inflammatory effect. Devitt-Lee explains further:

> "Imagine trying to power a car by simply lighting a fuel tank on fire. That's way too much energy. A cell can't handle the microscopic equivalent of an explosion, so the cell must use finesse to harness this energy...Although mitochondria allow energy to be accessed at a measured pace in relatively small quantities, the process of cellular respiration, whereby cells extract energy from nutrients, still can be damaging. High-energy electrons offload their energy in a multitude of complicated steps, until the lower-energy electron is finally released onto an oxygen molecule."[19]

The U.S. government currently has a patent on the antioxidant and neuroprotective properties of CBD. This patent illustrates the great hypocrisy of federal drug policy. U.S. policy toward medicinal cannabis is both unscientific and counterproductive and flies in the face of 4,000 years of medical history, 25,000 published peer-reviewed articles on cannabis, cannabinoids, and the ECS, thousands and thousands of basic science studies, and the experience of tens of thousands of physicians and millions of patients. Nevertheless, the present U.S. drug policy maintains that cannabis has "no known medical value." [20]

---

[19] Ibid.
[20] The United States of America Department of Justice Drug Enforcement Agency. *The Drug Enforcement Agency Position on Marijuana.* (Washington D.C, April 2013), page 1.

CHAPTER 5
HUMAN BRAIN

Reptilian Brain (Midbrain)

The human brain is composed of three distinct parts: the neocortex, the midbrain, often referred to as the "reptilian brain," and the limbic system, which helps integrate the reptilian brain with the neocortex. From primitive life forms to humans, all mammals ontologically incorporate the old reptilian brain, which is the oldest part of the brain. The midbrain controls primitive functions such as fight or flight and is involved in life or death decisions.

Research suggests that in humans the reptilian brain is important in the expression of obsessive-compulsive behavior, personal day-to-day rituals, superstitious acts, and conformity to old ways of doing things.

Neocortex

The neocortex is the most recently evolved part of the brain. The human brain has two large cerebral hemispheres, a characteristic shared by primates, which play a role in rational, higher order thinking. The cerebral hemispheres contribute to the development of human language, abstract thought, imagination, and consciousness, which have enabled the development of human cultures.

Modulation of Neural Input

Excessive, rapid neurotransmission likely contributes to the etiology of bipolar disorder, PTSD, ADD/ADHD, seizure disorder, migraines, explosive anger disorder, and IBS to name a few medical conditions related to speed of neural transmission. The body has mechanisms to help control

Parts of the Brain Affected by Cannabinoids

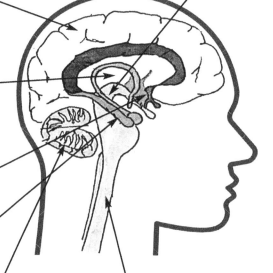

REPTILIAN BRAIN/MIDBRAIN
The oldest part of the brain. Critical for survival instincts (flight or fight). Critical for reproductive functions. Perceives everything as black and white, life or death.

CEREBRAL CORTEX
Evolutionarily the most recent. Plays a role in memory, thinking, perceptual awareness, and consciousness.

LIMBIC SYSTEM
Responsible for emotion, feeling and empathy.

HYPOTHALAMUS
Governs metabolic processes.

HIPPOCAMPUS
Central to memory storage and recall.

CEREBELLUM
Governs coordination and muscle control.

BRAIN STEM
Controls many basic functions including arousal, vomiting reflex, blood pressure, heart rate, and respiration. (NOTE: cannabis has little or no effect on the brain stem because it contains few or no CB1 receptors)

sensory overload. This is evidenced by the fact that 70% of our brain exists to slow down or modulate the other 30%. This modulation is mediated by a complex system of neurochemical and electrical on-off switches and regulators. The ECS is one of the brain's mechanisms that contributes to performing this modulatory role.

CHAPTER 6
HOMEOSTASIS

Homeostasis is defined as "the tendency toward a relatively stable equilibrium between interdependent elements, especially as maintained by physiological processes."[21] The ECS plays an important role in homeostasis and helps to regulate essential brain and body functions like pain, mood, digestion, sleep and appetite, among others.

Retired University of Colorado biology professor Dr. Robert Melamede has written extensively about the effect of cannabinoids and cannabis on homeostasis. He states, "Endocannabinoids are believed to have their evolutionary origins 600 million years in the past. Over the past decade and a half, since the identification of cannabinoid receptors, research into the cannabinoid system has grown exponentially."[22]

Melamede further states, "Endocannabinoids are marijuana-like compounds that have their origins hundreds of millions of years in the evolutionary past. They serve as fundamental modulators of energy homeostasis in many multicellular organisms, including all vertebrates. They have widespread biological activities that may often be attributed to their ability to minimize the negative consequences of free radicals."[23]

---

[21] Oxford Dictionary. "Definition of homeostasis in English."
https://en.oxforddictionaries.com/definition/homeostasis/.
[22] Melamede, Robert. "Endocannabinoids: multi-scaled, global homeostatic regulators of cells and society." In *Unifying Themes in Complex Systems*, pp. 219-226. Springer, Berlin, Heidelberg, 2010.
[23] Ibid.

CHAPTER 7
CONSTITUENTS AND CHEMICAL CHARACTERISTICS OF CANNABIS

Cannabis contains at least 512 different molecules, including flavonoids, terpenoids and cannabinoids.[24]

- There are over 100 cannabinoids and another 200-plus terpenes in cannabis.
- Cannabinoids are 21-carbon molecules that either stimulate or block CB1 or CB2 receptors.
- Terpenes are the molecules that give different varieties of cannabis their distinctive odors and they also are largely responsible for the effects of different cultivars.
- The main psychoactive substance is delta-9-tetrahydrocannabinol (THC), but at least 112 other cannabinoids synthesized by the plant have been identified as pyrolysis products of the plant. These include; cannabinol (CBN), cannabidiol (CBD), cannabigerol (CBG), and cannabichromene (CBC), as well as tetrahydrocannabinol (THC).
- Cannabis plant matter also contains chlorophyll, coloring matter (flavonoids), volatile oils, green resin, albumen, lignin, sugars, and salts such as potassium nitrate, silica, and phosphates, among other molecules.

---

[24] Aizpurua-Olaizola, Oier, Umut Soydaner, Ekin Öztürk, Daniele Schibano, Yilmaz Simsir, Patricia Navarro, Nestor Etxebarria, and Aresatz Usobiaga. "Evolution of the cannabinoid and terpene content during the growth of Cannabis sativa plants from different chemotypes." *Journal of Natural Products* 79, no. 2 (2016): 324-331.

There are over 500 different identifiable chemical constituents known to exist in cannabis. The most distinctive and specific class of compounds are the cannabinoids, 113 of which have been identified.

Other constituents of the plant are:

Aldehydes (13)
Amino acids (18)
Elements (9)
Enzymes (2)
Fatty acids (22)
Flavonoids (21)
Glycoproteins (6)
Hydrocarbons (50)
Ketones (13)
Lactones (1)
Nitrogenous compounds (27 known)
Non-cannabinoid phenols (25)
Pigments (2)
Proteins (3)
Simple acids (21)
Simple alcohols (7)
Simple esters (12)
Steroids (11)
Sugars and related compounds (34)
Terpenes (20)
Vitamins (1) [Vitamin A]

Understanding the basic chemistry of cannabis began with T. & H. Smith's declaration that the soporific, sleep-inducing, calmative, anti-anxiety, and other properties resided in the cannabis resin (1846). Personne (1857) thought the activity of the drug depended upon its volatile oil.[25] At the time it was known that vapor from cannabis could be stupefying. He succeeded in separating the oil into two parts—into a fluid known as cannabene ($C18H20$) and a crystallized solid known as cannabene hydride ($C18H22$).[26]

---

[25] Personne,, M. Jacques. "Rapport sur le concours relative d l'analyse du chanure, présenté au nom de la Société de Pharmacie." *Journal de Pharmacie et de Chimie* 31, 1857.

[26] "The Next Big Brain Cancer Drug Could Come from Marijuana," *Fortune*, February 2017, fortune.com/2017/02107/gw-pharmaceuticals-marijuana-brain-cancer.

There was a gap of well over a hundred years before the chemistry of the active constituents of the plant began to be well characterized. THC was first isolated and its molecular structure characterized in 1964 by Israeli scientist Raphael Mechoulam, Ph.D. THC is the most euphorigenic of the cannabinoids and along with CBD one of the most therapeutically useful constituents of the plant. The first modern, formal physiologic research on cannabis (that we are aware of) was done in 1968 at Harvard by Dr. Andrew Weil, now chair of the Center of Integrative Medicine at the University of Arizona.[27]

The first modern medicinal study on a cannabinoid was done in 1947 by Ramsey and Davis, who found that synthetic THC was useful for treating epilepsy. Many human double-blind research studies on medicinal application of cannabis were done in the first decade of the 21st century in the United Kingdom by GW Pharmaceuticals and in California under the auspices of the California Medical Cannabis Research Center (CMCR) headquartered at the University of California at San Diego (UCSD) School of Medicine. Eighteen FDA approved clinical studies done at four University of California medical schools under the auspice of the CMCR scientifically confirmed several of the historical medicinal uses of cannabis, such as analgesia, muscle relaxant, anti-depressant, anti-anxiety and treatment of neuro-degenerative disease.[28]

Cannabinoids

There are over 100 cannabinoids in cannabis.[29] THC is considered to be the most pharmacologically active constituent of cannabis sativa. In addition to THC, other cannabinoids such as cannabidiol (CBD), cannabinol (CBN) and cannabigerol (CBG) have drawn considerable attention for their therapeutic application.

---

[27] Weil, Andrew. *The Natural Mind: An Investigation of Drugs and the Higher Consciousness* (Houghton Mifflin Harcourt, 1972).

[28] Center for Medicinal Cannabis Research (CMRC), "Report to Legislature and Governor of the State of California Presenting Findings Pursuant to California Senate Bill 847 Which Created the CMCR and Provided State Funding". February 11, 2010.

[29] Aizpurua-Olaizola, Op. cit.

Scientific research has generated interest in cannabinoids for treatment of cancer. In vitro studies by GW Pharmaceuticals have determined that the cannabinoids CBN, CBD, and CBG are effective in inhibiting aggressive cancers.[30] They found that a synergistic increase in both the antiproliferative and apoptotic (cell-killing) activity of cannabinoids can be produced by combining specific ratios of CB1 and CB2 receptor agonists with non-psychotropic cannabinoids[31] GW recently completed a study on glioblastoma using 25mg THC, 25g CBD three times a day. The study group experienced an 83 percent one-year survival rating compared to a 53 percent one-year survival rating for those with conventional treatment alone.[32]

Cannabinoids have been shown to have benefit for treating neurodegenerative diseases and movement disorders like Multiple Sclerosis, Parkinson's Disease, Cerebellar degeneration, seizure disorders and Alzheimer's Disease. An intriguing area of cannabinoid research lies within the field of

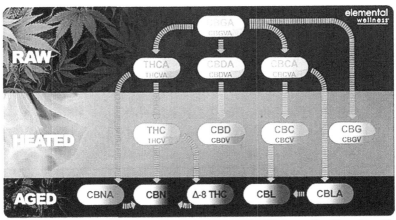

http://cannagramma.com/wp-content/uploads/2015/10/UnderstandingCannabis.pdf

---

[30] G. Velasco, PhD, C. Sanchez, PhD, and M. Guzman, "Anti-Cancer Mechanisms of Cannabinoids," *Current Oncology*, March 23, 2016.

[31] GW Pharmaceuticals Archives, "Positive Results in Phase 2 Proof of Concept Study in Glioma," February 7, 2017.

[32] Ibid, GW Pharmaceuticals Archive.

Alzheimer's disease prevention. Alzheimer's disease is caused by the aggregation of amyloid plaque, promoting the production of neurofibrillary entanglement. The presence of cannabinoids prohibits the aggregation of amyloid plaque.[33]

For more specific information about state of science investigating cannabinoids, please see *Appendix B: Resources on Cannabinoids* in the back of the book.

Here are some examples of cannabinoids and a few of their therapeutic properties:

- **CBC (Cannabichromene)**
  First discovered in 1966, CBC has not been extensively studied. There are no more than 75 published papers on PubMed that make specific references to CBC.

  A 2009 review of cannabichromene and other non-psychotropic cannabinoids revealed medical uses of CBC. It can act as a pain reliever, sleep aid, anti-spasmatic, anti-inflammatory, antimicrobial, anti-fungal, anti-cancer agent and promoter of bone growth. Freshly harvested, dry cannabis contains significant quantities of CBC.

- **CBG (Cannabigerol)**
  CBG has anti-cancer and anti-inflammatory properties. In addition, it acts as a sleep aid and slows bacterial growth.

- **THC (Δ-9 Tetrahydrocannabinol)**
  The most well-known and the most euphorigenic of the cannabinoids, THC has anti-cancer, anti-nauseant, analgesic, muscle relaxant, neuroprotective, anti-inflammatory, pain relieving, appetite stimulating, and anti-seizure properties.

- **CBN (Cannabinol)**
  First isolated in 1896, CBN is a product of THC degradation. Found in cannabis in minute quantities, it weakly binds to humans' endogenous cannabinoid

---

[33] Romero J. *Cannabinoids and Alzheimer's Disease.* Presented at the Eighth National Clinical Conference on Cannabis Therapeutics; 2014; Portland, OR

receptors. CBN is a mildly psychotropic cannabinoid that potentiates the effects of THC. There are over 500 published papers in the scientific literature specific to CBN. Several articles document CBN's therapeutic potential, which includes its ability to induce sleep, to ease pain and spasticity, to delay ALS (Lou Gehrig's Disease) symptoms, to increase appetite, and to halt the spread of certain antibiotic-resistant pathogens like methicillin-resistant Staphylococcus aureus (MRSA). Combining THC with CBN yields enhanced sedating effects.

Health Effects of Marijuana	THC	THC-A	THC-V	CBN	CBD	CBD-A	CBC	CBC-A	CBG	CBG-A	Benefits
Pain relief	X			X	X		X		X		Analgesic
Reduces inflammation		X			X	X	X		X		Anti-inflamatory
Supresses appetite			X								Anoretic
Stimulates appetite	X								X		Appetite stimulant
Reduces vomiting and nausea	X				X						Antimetic
Reduces contractions of small intestine		X			X						Intestinal antiprokinetic
Relieves anxiety					X						Anxiolytic
Tranquilizing / psychosis management					X						Antipsychotic
Reduces seizures and convulsions			X	X	X						Antiepileptic
Suppresses muscle spasms	X				X						Antispasmodic
Aides sleep				X	X						Anti-insomnia
Reduces efficacy of immune system	X				X						Immunosuppresive
Reduces blood sugar levels					X		X				Anti-diabetic
Prevents nervous system degeneration	X				X		X				Neuroprotective
Treats psoriasis					X						Antipsioratic
Reduces risk of artery blockage					X						Anti-ischemic
Kills or slows bacteria growth					X				X	X	Anti-bacterial
Treats fungal infection									X	X	Anti-fungal
Inhibits cell growth in tumours / cancer	X		X		X	X	X		X		Anti-proliferative
Promotes bone growth			X		X		X		X	X	Bone-stimulant

https://s3-us-west-2.amazonaws.com/greenflowermedia/wp-content/uploads/2015/10/rev7.jpg

- **THCV (Tetrahydrocannabivarin)**
  Medicinal properties of THCV include anorectic, bone-stimulant, and anti-epileptic properties. It is currently being researched as a treatment for metabolic disorders, including diabetes.

- **CBD (Cannabidiol)**
  CBD was first identified in 1940 and its specific chemical structure determined in 1963. Many researchers believe that CBD is the cannabinoid that

possesses the greatest therapeutic potential. Studies suggest a wide range of possible therapeutic effects of cannabidiol on several conditions, including Alzheimer's disease, Parkinson's disease, nausea, cancer, cerebral ischemia, diabetes, rheumatoid arthritis, and other inflammatory diseases.[34]

A Brief Word About CBD:
CBD is Psychoactive but Not Psychotropic

CBD is often referred to as "non-psychoactive", but this is scientifically inaccurate. CBD is never intoxicating, but it is always psychoactive. CBD crosses the blood-brain barrier, alters mood, and helps alleviate neurological conditions such as epilepsy. However, unlike THC, CBD is "non-psychotropic," meaning it does not cause the euphoria and/or dysphoria that can accompany a THC "high". The higher presence of CBD in high-THC cannabis mediates the undesirable side effect of dysphoria.[35] In my experience, CBD decreases the euphoria of THC by about one-third. For example, a 1:1 ratio of THC to CBD at 30 mg each will cause about the same amount of euphoria as 20 mg of just plain THC (dronabinol).

At one time, it was believed that CBD did not directly affect the CB1 or CB2 receptors. It exerts an effect on THC signals because it has an allosteric binding to CB1 receptors. This appears to be responsible for the partial decrease of the euphoric effect of Δ-9 THC. Some references state that CBD suppresses the enzyme fatty acid amide hydroxylase ("FAAH").[36] This enzyme metabolizes anandamide and thus potentiates the endocannabinoid effects.

[34] Zuardi, Antonio Waldo. "Cannabidiol: from an inactive cannabinoid to a drug with wide spectrum of action." *Revista brasileira de psiquiatria 30*, no. 3 (2008): 271-280.
[35] Russo, Ethan, and Geoffrey W. Guy. "A tale of two cannabinoids: the therapeutic rationale for combining tetrahydrocannabinol and cannabidiol." *Medical hypotheses66*, no. 2 (2006): 234-246.
[36] "Cannabis: Why is CBD Non Psychoactive?" *Harmony.*
https://meetharmony.com/2016/10/24/cbd-non-psychoactive/.

CBD acts as a pain reliever, sleep aid, relieves spasms, reduces anxiety, is an anti-inflammatory, vaso-relaxant, it reduces seizures, reduces blood sugar levels, reduces small intestine contractions, promotes bone growth, slows bacterial growth, inhibits cancer cell growth, is neuroprotective, antiemetic and contains bone-stimulating properties.

A team at the University of Reading School of Pharmacy in the United Kingdom discovered that CBD has the potential to prevent seizures with few side effects, such as uncontrollable shaking, which accompanies many existing prescription anti-epileptic drugs. CBD was also found to work as an adjuvant with other pharmaceutical treatment to control epilepsy.[37]

Cannabinoids in Acid Form

The major cannabinoid constituents in raw cannabis come in the form of acids (e.g., THCa, CBDa, etc). Preliminary research suggests the acidic cannabinoids hold most of the anti-inflammatory properties that cannabis has to offer, but much more research is needed. Acidic cannabinoids also show promise in the treatment of irritable bowel syndrome and Crohn's Disease.

Cannabinoids in the acid form go through a chemical change called decarboxylation. This decarboxylation forms their non-acidic counterparts. This can happen over time with drying or with heat. When cannabis is smoked, the heat causes the acidic cannabinoids to decarboxylate (i.e., removal or loss of a carboxyl group).

THCa (THC acid) does NOT cause euphoria. This is probably because the carboxyl group affects the way the THCa molecule fits into the CB1 receptor. Due to THCa's carboxyl group, juicing the raw plant allows a person to consume very high doses of THC without dysphoria. In order

---

[37] Geffrey, Alexandra L., Sarah F. Pollack, Patricia L. Bruno, and Elizabeth A. Thiele. "Drug-drug interaction between clobazam and cannabidiol in children with refractory epilepsy." *Epilepsia56*, no. 8 (2015): 1246-1251.

to avoid dysphoria some clinicians have recommended juicing. The challenge for patients who would benefit from juicing the plant is that juicing requires considerable plant product for a glass of juice. Currently, most states limit the amount of plants that a patient is allowed to grow, thus limiting the extent to which this recommendation can be followed.

CHAPTER 8
TERPENES

Terpenes are ubiquitous, with over 20,000 currently known to exist in nature. Terpenes can be differentiated by the number of repeating units of a 5-carbon molecule called isoprene. They are essential oils that exist as monoterpenes, diterpenes, or sesquiterpenes.

Terpenes are aromatic molecules that are more volatile than cannabinoids, so their presence is more closely related to the freshness and temperature of cannabis. The fresher and cooler the cannabis, the better the terpenes are preserved. Over 200 terpenes have been isolated in cannabis and each botanical variety of cannabis contains a unique terpene chemical profile. This gives each cannabis plant a distinctive aroma and flavor.

Therapeutic Effect of Terpenes

Terpenes have therapeutic value in their own right and are found in many plants: citrus fruit, flowers, pepper and other spices. For centuries spices have been used therapeutically based on their terpene profile. Here are a few examples:

Myrcene

Myrcene is also found in hops and mangoes. Myrcene acts as a sleep aid, sedative hypnotic, and muscle relaxant. It also has analgesic, anti-inflammatory, antipsychotic, antispasmodic, and possibly anti-cancer properties.

Pinene

Some texts say Pinene is the most common naturally occurring terpene. Its medical uses include anti-inflammatory, gastroprotective, anti-bacterial and anti-anxiety properties. This is likely one of the reasons a walk in a pine forest can be so relaxing. It also acts as a bronchodilator and an acetylcholinesterase inhibitor which can aid memory. Pinene, along with chlorophyll, accounts for cannabis' familiar green color. It is associated with pine trees and turpentine. Pinene has been found to provide a limiting effect of THC's euphorogenic effect.

Limonene

Limonene is often found in citrus and has anti-anxiety, antidepressant, gastroprotective, anti-microbial, and antispasmodic properties in some strains. Pinene and Limonene, have been found to provide a limiting effect of THC's euphorogenic effect. Limonene gives cannabis an aroma of citrus.

It can be used to help prevent and treat cancer and has anxiolytic and immunostimulant properties. Its anti-inflammatory properties aid with inflammatory conditions, autoimmune diseases, connective tissue disorders such as degenerative arthritis, bursitis, rheumatoid arthritis, systemic lupus, ankylosing spondylitis, and fibromyalgia. It also helps kill tumor cells and aids healing in skin tissue by promoting cellular regeneration.

Linalool

Linalool is also found in an array of flowers, most notably lavender, as well as in mint, cinnamon, and some fungi. It also has anti-anxiety, (anxiolytic) sedative, anti-convulsive, analgesic, anti-neoplastic, anesthetic, and antipsychotic properties.

Phytol

Phytol is commonly found in green tea and increases GABA via SSADH inhibition. This causes it to be a relaxant and aids in lowering cholesterol.

ß-Caryophyllene

Beta-caryophyllene is found in the essential oil of black pepper, oregano, other edible herbs, many green leafy vegetables, and cannabis. It has a hoppy flavor/aroma and has gastroprotective, anti-inflammatory, analgesic, anti-fungal, and possibly anti-cancer properties. It decreases platelet aggregation and may be an effective treatment for autoimmune disorders.

This terpene binds directly to the CB2 receptors found in the immune system. The CB2 binding was documented in 2008 by Swiss scientist Jürg Gertsch, who described B-

	Linalool	Myrcene	Limonene	Caryophyllene	Alpha Pinene
SCENT PROFILE	FLORAL SPICE	WOOD & EARTHY	CITRUS ORANGE	PEPPER & CLOVE	PINE & RESIN
PLANTS	cinamon & lavender	mango & hops	lemon & rosemary	cloves & peppercorn	salvia plant & pine needles

caryophyllene as a "dietary cannabinoid."[38]

Entourage Effect/ Phytopharmaceutical Synergy

In 1999, Israeli scientist Dr. Raphael Mechoulam (who in 1964 isolated and characterized the chemical structure of THC) postulated what he called the "Entourage Effect" (aka "The Ensemble Effect"). This term describes the combined effect of all the therapeutic constituents of the cannabis plant acting together,[39] meaning the presence of all cannabinoids in the plant are needed to balance each other naturally. "Whole plant medicine" is a term used to describe cannabis medicines utilizing the full spectrum of naturally occurring therapeutic molecules cannabis has to offer.

A glimpse of the properties and benefits of some cannabinoids and terpenes is provided above. These are just a

---

38 Gertsch, Jürg, Marco Leonti, Stefan Raduner, Ildiko Racz, Jian-Zhong Chen, Xiang-Qun Xie, Karl-Heinz Altmann, Meliha Karsak, and Andreas Zimmer. "Beta-caryophyllene is a dietary cannabinoid." *Proceedings of the National Academy of Sciences* 105, no. 26 (2008): 9099-9104.

39 Ben-Shabat, Shimon, Ester Fride, Tzviel Sheskin, Tsippy Tamiri, Man-Hee Rhee, Zvi Vogel, Tiziana Bisogno, Luciano De Petrocellis, Vincenzo Di Marzo, and Raphael Mechoulam. "An entourage effect: inactive endogenous fatty acid glycerol esters enhance 2-arachidonoyl-glycerol cannabinoid activity." *European Journal of Pharmacology* 353, no. 1 (1998): 23-31

few of the therapeutic terpene and cannabinoid properties found in cannabis. The entourage effect is thought to improve the therapeutic outcome over the use of any one isolated constituent of the known 512 molecules found in the plant. Use of any one constituent by itself is like throwing the nutrient-rich rice husk away and eating the least nutritional part.

This entourage effect meets the definition of phytopharmaceutical synergy set forth by Wagner and Ulrich-Merzenich. They say that to have successful phyto-pharmaceutical synergy such as with cannabis, there are four basic theoretical mechanisms:

1. Affect multiple targets within the body
2. Improve active ingredients absorption
3. Overcome bacterial defense mechanisms
4. Minimize adverse side effects.[40]

Terpenes as Examples of the Entourage Effect

The best evidence of the entourage effect comes from renowned cannabis researchers Dr. Mechoulam and Dr. Grinspoon. Dr. Ethan Russo, former GW Pharmaceuticals North American medical consultant, now medical director of Phytecs, explained the entourage effect in a 2011 paper published in the *British Journal of Pharmacology*. He reviewed some possible interactions amongst various cannabinoids and terpenes.[41] The article used the terpene a-pinene as an example.

The article described a study that suggests a-pinene might help preserve acetylcholine, which has been implicated in memory formation. Russo suggests that "One main side effect of THC is short-term memory impairment...That can be prevented if there's pinene in the cannabis." Thus, a-pinene helps counteract compromised cognition and memory that might be associated with THC.

[40] Wagner, Hildebert, and G. Ulrich-Merzenich. "Synergy research: approaching a new generation of phytopharmaceuticals." Phytomedicine 16, no. 2-3 (2009): 97-110.
[41] Russo, Ethan B. "Taming THC: potential cannabis synergy and phytocannabinoid-terpenoid entourage effects." *British Journal of Pharmacology* 163, no. 7 (2011): 1344-1364.

Myrcene can reduce resistance in the blood-brain barrier, enabling easier passage of other beneficial chemicals.

Many have found that ß-caryophyllene, a terpene found in black pepper, may bring a person down from dysphoria. Two tablespoons of black pepper stirred into a glass of water and swallowed can help counteract THC-induced dysphoria. Interestingly, a combination of terpenes, pinene, myrcene, and caryophyllene helps reduce anxiety.

Linalool and Limonene

Mixing linalool and limonene with CBG shows promise in the treatment of MRSA, while a combination of linalool, limonene, and CBD has been shown to be an anti-acne treatment.

Due to the Schedule I status of cannabis, the federal government has put research out of reach for most scientists. As a result, there is no hard evidence confirming the entourage effect. Like so many aspects of the ECS, cannabis, and cannabinoids, we have just scratched the surface of understanding. "With marijuana, most of what you're dealing with is anecdotal evidence," Mowgli Holmes says. "But the truth is there's very, very little data."

Holmes is the chief scientific officer at cannabis genome-mapping company Phylos Bioscience. He adds, "We can't do very basic studies about what's really true...But [when] you have thousands and thousands of people reporting the same thing...It gets hard to ignore."[44]

It is true that some double-blind clinical trials have been conducted to investigate the effects of terpenes as well as cannabinoids found in cannabis other than THC, but there is a large gap to fill. Future studies should provide even more evidence of the entourage effect.

---

44 Chen, Angus. "Scientists say most marijuana strains act basically the same." *PBS Newshour*. April 20, 2017.
.https://www.pbs.org/newshour/science/character-favorite-marijuana-strain-may-head/.id.

CHAPTER 9
DOSING

Plant Potency

In *The Botany of Desire* (2001), Michael Pollan highlights the gradual evolution of the cannabis plant over millennia.[45] Botanical changes in recent years have been influenced by growers producing cannabis largely for adult use with the understanding that THC was responsible for all of the plant's effects. Consequently, the percentage of THC has arguablly increased several-fold.[46] Until the 1960s, the average THC content in cannabis plants usually ranged from 0.3% to 4% depending on the climate, soil, growing conditions, and handling after harvest. In the present day, the THC content of the flower can be up to about 20%. Some say that since THC concentration is variable and technology has improved comparing the average THC content of the 60s to today is comparing apples to oranges.[47] THC levels may be up to 90 percent or more in some extractions.

According to the 1997 House of Lords Select Committee on Science and Technology Report, the concentration of THC in the late 1990s ranged from 1-5%, for plants grown in North America.[48] They wrote that stock coming from Panama, Mexico, and especially Thailand, frequently yielded the highest values. This is because THC production is a direct response to UV-B light, which there is a lot more of around the

[45] Pollan, Michael. *The Botany of Desire: A Plant's-Eye View of the World*. New York: Random House, 2001

[46] Lafrance, Adrienne. "Was Marijuana Really Less Potent in the 60s?." *The Atlantic*. March 6, 2015.

[47] Ibid.

[48] House of Lords. "Science of Technology - Ninth Report." United Kingdom Parliament. November 4, 1998.

equator. For instance, in 1981, Baker et al. found the THC value in the range 1.0-10.6% in cannabis and 6.0-12.5% in cannabis resin. A one-gram cannabis cigarette containing 10 mg of THC (1%) is considered psychoactive. Hashish resin may have up to 60% THC by weight.[49] More recently, THC value in cannabis as high as 20% (or more) have been achieved. While occasional claims of higher percentages have been claimed, according to Jeff Raber of The WERC Shop testing labs, these numbers are suspect due to botanical and testing limitations.[50]

The concentration or percentage of each of the 512 constituents in cannabis varies from one variety to another and even from plant to plant within the same family. Unlike pharmaceutical medicines, the cannabis plant is a living organism with unique DNA from seed to seed, and the end product concentrations are both a result of nature (the plant's genetics) and nurture (the conditions under which it is grown).

By bureaucratic fiat, plants grown for hemp fiber must have a THC concentration of less than 0.3% THC. A 2005 report from the United Kingdom says that the Dutch organization Maripharm produces medical grade cannabis which has a consistent content of THC 10.7± 0.1 percent.[51]

The 1997 House of Lords Science and Technology Committee Report stated that at that time in the U.S., "Cannabis resin joints" with tobacco had on average approximately 150 mg of resin, ranging from around 50 mg to 350 mg. Herbal cannabis "joints" with tobacco contain an average of around 200 mg cannabis, although amounts vary considerably. A minority of herbal cannabis users, mainly those who grow their own, smoke cannabis in neat cigarettes containing 500 mg to one gram of plant material.[52]

---

[49] Baker, P. B., K. R. Bagon, and T. A. Gough. "Variation in the THC content in illicitly imported cannabis products." *Bulletin on Narcotics* 32, no. 4 (1980): 47-54.

[50] Rappold, R. Scott. "Jeffrey Raber of The Werc Shop." *Culture Magazine*. February 4, 2016. http://ireadculture.com/industry-insider/.

[51] Gorter, Robert W., Mario Butorac, Eloy Pulido Cobian, and Willem van der Sluis. "Medical use of cannabis in the Netherlands." *Neurology* 64, no. 5 (2005): 917-919.

[52] House of Lords. "Science of Technology - Ninth Report." United Kingdom Parliament. November 4, 1998.

Investigational New Drug (IND) Program

This is a good practical contemporary basis for speculation regarding dosage. The federal IND program started in 1978 with a single glaucoma patient, Robert Randall. The program was a result of a legal agreement to preserve Randall's eyesight. At first the cannabis was sent to and monitored by a Johns Hopkins assistant professor. When the professor moved on to another institution, the government was finally forced, by a historic 1978 court decision, to provide Randall with his sight-saving cannabis. This judicial decree established the IND program. This program provided Randall, and subsequently 14 other patients, the amount of cannabis necessary to obtain a therapeutic result for their individual medical conditions.

The federal government provides seven to nine pounds of cannabis cigarettes per year to IND patients. The program was closed to new participants in 1992, but 15 patients who were already part of the program were grandfathered in for life. As of December 2017, the federal government still supplies four patients with 300 4% THC cannabis cigarettes, each containing 0.9 of a gram of ground cannabis flower.[53]

In 2004 Dr. Ethan Russo and Mary Lynn Mathre, RN did a comprehensive health study of the history and physical status of four of the then seven surviving IND patients. Other than their underlying medical problem for which they were taking cannabis to treat, they were in otherwise normal health for people of their ages and genders.[54]

Here is information on three (3) of these IND study patients.

---

[53] "Free pot? Federal Program Ships Marijuana to Four." CBS News.
https://www.cbsnews.com/pictures/free-pot-federal-program-ships-marijuana-to-four/.
[54] Russo, Ethan, Mary Lynn Mathre, Al Byrne, Robert Velin, et. al. "Chronic Cannabis Use in the Compassionate Investigational New Drug Program: An Examination of Benefits and Adverse Effects of Legal Clinical Cannabis." *Journal of Cannabis Therapeutics* 2(1), 2002

Age/Gender	Qualifying Condition	IND Approval- Years of Cannabis Usage	Daily Cannabis/THC Content
62, female	Glaucoma	(1988) 39 years	8 grams (0.28 oz), 3.8%
52, male	Nail-Patella Syndrome	(1989) 41 years	7 grams (0.25 oz), 3.75%
48, female	Multiple Sclerosis	(1989) 41 years	9 grams (0.32 oz), 3.5%

How Much THC Does a Cannabis Cigarette (Joint) Deliver?

THC dosage in cannabis cigarettes can be reasonably determined with simple math (e.g. a one-gram cannabis cigarette containing 10% THC cannabis has 100 mg of THC). This, however, is not the amount that is delivered to the patient. Smoking destroys 30% of available THC. Therefore, when smoked, a cannabis cigarette delivers no more than 30% of the THC it contains to the blood stream. An additional amount is lost to the air and still more is left in the butt (stub/roach) so more like 16-17% of that is absorbed.[55] Smoked cannabis is more efficient than oral-consumed cannabis for immediate relief of nausea or pain despite the wasted THC.[56] When ingested orally, 85% of THC is metabolized through the liver on the first pass to the very psychotropic 11-hydroxy-THC.

Historically, there has long been desire for standardization of medicinal cannabis. Lack of modern testing technology in the early 20th century and the plant's subsequent illegal status has impeded standardization. All that has changed since 1999. Now, when grown under pharmaceutical conditions, a standardized dose is possible. With the advent of Sativex

---

[55] Roffman, R.A. and R. Stephens, eds. *Cannabis Dependence: Its Nature, Consequences, and Treatment*. Cambridge University Press, 2006.
[56] House of Lords. "Science of Technology - Ninth Report." United Kingdom Parliament. November 4, 1998.

(nabiximols), Epidiolex (high CBD, low THC) and Marinol (dronabinol), we now have available to us medication containing standardized, reproducible amounts of THC and in the case of nabiximols and Epidiolex, CBD. (Note: While Marinol has been on the market since the mid-1980s, it is not cannabis. Marinol is only synthetic THC.)

Ratios of THC to CBD

Research has proven the therapeutic value of many of the cannabinoids, but there is still much to learn about the effect of varying ratios and amounts of different cannabinoids. Many cannabinoid medicine practitioners are curious as to what the optimal ratio of THC to CBD is, but this is still unknown. The reason that this is hard to nail down is because of human variability, plant variability and complexity, and lack of research. Dosage, cannabinoid ratios, and the therapeutic contribution of terpenes are all currently being looked at. Plant DNA studies are also in progress. While more research, both clinical and basic science, is needed, this should not prevent us from acting on our current state of knowledge.

What are THC- and CBD-only Medicines?

Some patients have found that either THC alone or CBD alone can be effective therapeutic agents; however, they are rarely if ever as effective as the two together. There are several prescription THC-only medicines on the market, which include Marinol (dronabinol) and Cesamet (nabilone). These are legal, FDA approved pharmaceuticals which contain only synthetic THC. They are approved to ease cancer treatment-related nausea and appetite suppression. Not surprisingly, these synthetic THC pharmaceuticals are more expensive than cannabis, they do not work as well, and have more side effects. They do not benefit from the entourage effect, but they do have therapeutic application.

You can also purchase CBD-only products, but like THC-only products they do not engage the entourage effect. CBD-only medicines came to prominence following a CNN documentary by Dr. Sanja Gupta demonstrating the use of a non-euphorigenic cannabis cultivar "Charlotte's Web" as a very effective anti-epileptic. Interestingly, in my experience CBD-only or high-CBD strains do not work as well as the whole plant to treat epilepsy. There has been general agreement by clinicians that neither THC or CBD by themselves nor just the two together are as effective as the whole plant.

Because of the entourage effect many clinical experts recommend using a whole plant extract rather than a single isolate such as CBD or THC. Even very low amounts of THC can contribute to beneficial medical effects. In most instances the therapeutic benefits of CBD are enhanced by using 1-2 mg. of THC. This would not produce euphoria but would enhance the entourage effect.

We need to guard against the "euphoriphobia" that some patients have. These are patients who are adamant about not feeling high. In some instances THC is essential to getting the true therapeutic effect of cannabis. While the reason for having such a feeling may be from a bad experience in the past such as paranoia or anxiety. This is usually from at one time ingesting too much THC (e.g., more than 10 mg.)

Dose Experience with Patent Medicines

Some light may be shed on appropriate contemporary dosing by looking at the doses recommended in cannabis-containing patent medicines popular in the late 19th century and early 20th century. In the early years of the 20th century, cannabis was widely available as a medical treatment. It was used as a nerve sedative and an analgesic, prescribed for migraine, neuralgia and dysmenorrhea among other indications. The preparations available were an alcoholic tincture and aqueous extract. The suggested doses were:

Extractum Cannabis Indica (B.P., U.S.P.). Dose: 1-4 grams (15-60 mg.)
Extractum Cannabis Indica (B.P., U.S.P.). Dose: 1 gram (15 mg.)[57]

---

[57] Pharmacopeia, United States. "11th rev." .
http://antiquecannabisbook.com/Appendix/USP1942.htm/.

General Non-Scientific Adult Dose (AKA "Recreational" Dose)

Normal Adult Dosage of THC

Novice User	2.5-5 mg
Experienced/Moderate User	10-20 mg
Heavy Frequent User	25 mg +

Euphoria can usually begin to be felt at 10 mg of THC. Dysphoria may occur in sensitive patients at 15mg. However, tolerance can develop and may not occur with much higher dosages. Advice to the novice user: it is best to start with the respiratory route of administration due to the relative ease of dose titration. Start with a low dose and only slowly increase the dose balancing the desired therapeutic effect against any undesirable side effects.

Therapeutic Dose

It is difficult to stand on firm ground when determining appropriate cannabis dosage for a specific condition. This is due to lack of double blind studies, confounded by plant and human variability. Current research, animal and tissue culture studies plus clinical experience form the basis for speculation on dosage estimates and cannabinoid ratios. Many questions still need to be answered:

- How many milligrams of THC are effective for each person for different conditions?
- What is the correct THC/CBD ratio?
- What role do some (or all) of the cannabis plant's 113 cannabinoids play in providing therapeutic relief?
- What is the role of different terpenes in aiding treatment of different conditions?

This author's experience has demonstrated substantial variability in the THC dosage and/or THC/CBD ratio that patients respond favorably to for different conditions. This variability is due more to human genetic variability and tolerances determined by current and prior uses than to lack of plant standardization.

This does not mean cannabis should not be utilized as a medicine because we do know enough about dosing. Valuable knowledge has been gleaned from animal and tissue culture research as well as from clinical experience with cannabis and cannabinoids. The key is to approach cannabis in the same manner as other therapeutic agents. Individuals are all different, so as with many other therapeutic agents, we should start with a low dose and slowly increase the dose while assessing an appropriate balance between the side effects and the therapeutic benefits.

There are several cannabinoid and cannabis-based prescription medicines on the market in the world today. These include dronabinol and Nabilone. Nabiximols (Sativex) is approved for medical use in 24 countries and is a whole plant alcohol extract. Experience with these standardized cannabis and cannabinoid prescription preparations provide some guidance for dosage of cannabis.

Respiratory Dose
There is no "one size fits all" dose to generate euphoria. However, an effective dose of THC is usually considered to be between two and 40 milligrams when smoked, and between 20 and 90 milligrams when taken orally.[58] It has been my experience that with a 20 mg dose of dronabinol at least 30% of patients complain of dysphoria. For many conditions a dose of cannabis that contains 2-5 mg THC is a good place to start and is usually sufficient to obtain the desired therapeutic effect. If not effective, you may wish to add 2.5 mg CBD.

Under normal smoking conditions, 16 to 19% of the THC in the cannabis cigarette is consumed, the rest is pyrolyzed (burned) and wafts off in smoke. Smoking delivers different molecules to the body than vaping because it burns (oxidizes)

---

[58] Noyes, Russell, S. Brunk, David A. Baram, and Arthur Canter. "Analgesic Effect of Delta-9-Tetrahydrocannabinol." *The Journal of Clinical Pharmacology* 15, no. 2-3 (1975): 139-143.

the molecules in cannabis. This creates additional molecules to inhale besides just those produced naturally by the plant, and some of these are chemical constituents that can irritate the bronchial tree.

The respiratory route can also be achieved by vaporization. Vaporization (heating volatile oils until they enter the gas phase) delivers 70% fewer irritants to the bronchial tree and lungs than delivered by pyrolysis. With vaporization you do not get the oxidized compounds that are created with smoking.

Oral Dose

After prescribing THC (dronabinol) for hundreds of patients this author found it has provided a guide to dose ranges for many conditions. Dronabinol can then provide both the doctor and the patient a more specific dose range of THC to start at when beginning use with the whole plant. Information from using Nabiximols (Sativex), a widely studied, whole plant, alcohol extract with a 1:1 THC:CBD ratio provides evidence that clinicians can utilize.

After some trial and error with both dronabinol and cannabis recommendations, I have developed some standard dosage guidelines. These are meant to be general guidelines, not as firm numbers.

Analgesic Dose

Research by Noyes et al. in the 1970s found that 20 mg of THC was the therapeutic equivalent of 60 mg of codeine.[59] My experience is that cannabis, which contains 10-20 mg THC per dose, plus an equal or lesser amount of CBD, is often helpful for relieving pain. For analgesia I would suggest starting with a cannabis product containing 10 mg of THC along with 10 mg CBD three to four times per day. Then, if there are no adverse side effects and little or no pain relief response, try 15 mg THC and 15 mg CBD. According to a discussion with Deborah Malka, MD, PhD, she recommends never using more than a 1:1 ratio of THC to CBD for pain relief. Sativex, a 1:1 THC:CBD tincture, has been shown in

---

[59] Noyes, Op. cit.

clinical trials to treat intractable pain. Many terpenes have anti-inflammatory properties.

Anxiety Relief Dose

Relatively low doses of THC (in the 2.5-5 mg range two to three times a day), usually combined with CBD, can be helpful for controlling not only anxiety but some of the symptoms of autism spectrum disorder, social anxiety, ADD, ADHD and PTSD. A patient can use two to four times as much CBD as THC for anxiety relief, so 5-10 mg CBD is fine. Many terpenes also have anti-anxiety properties.

Treating Cancer

Lay healers who use Full Extract Cannabis Oil (FECO, aka Rick Simpson Oil or RSO) often start with a kilogram (2.2 pounds) of cannabis and do an alcohol extraction. Each lay healer has their own protocol. This is usually some variant of one to three grams per day of FECO for 60 or 90 days. These lay healers tend to recommend anywhere from 200 mg-700 mg of THC per day and the same dose range of CBD. The THC/CBD ratio differs from one healer to the next. As with many aspects of cannabis, and in common with many other medicines, more research is needed.

There are several constituents of the plant including CBN and CBG as well as THC and CBD that have been identified as having cancer cell killing properties. A combination of the plant's constituents is often superior to isolated compounds. Cannabinoids possess synergistic anti-cancer properties. Cannabis can prevent proliferation of cancer cells. Cannabis suppresses tumor angiogenesis and inhibits cancer adhesion and migration. It also induces apoptosis in cancer cells.

Anti-Proliferative Dose

The dosages suggested to kill cancer cells are quite high. Most patients will experience dysphoria for at least ten days and in many cases even longer. According to Dustin Sulak, DO, the goal is 5-25 mg/kg/day total cannabinoids divided TID-QID.

Due to medical legal constraints, treatment is usually provided by lay healters. While each one has their own slightly different, unique approach, the range is two to three grams/day of concentrated cannabis for 60-90 days followed by a lifetime maintenance dose of .5 to 1.0 gram/day of concentrated cannabis. By comparison 2.5 mg. of THC (dronabinol) can provide anxiety relief.

Not surprisingly it is very common that cancer patients treated with high THC cannabis have reported an unpleasant effect beyond euphoria to dysphoria and describe the effects specifically as anxiety and/or paranoia. While the side effects from cannabis are not as significant as those from conventional chemo and radiation, it has some very real side effects including nausea, vomiting as well as anxiety, dysphoria panic attacks and paranoia. There are several strategies for mitigating these side effects of the cannabis dose for cancer.

The rectal route of administration can help keep the high down. The use of cannabis suppositories helps decrease the onset and intensity of the high from the metabolic breakdown product and strong euphoriant 11 hydroxy THC. This is because the pelvic floor is served by three veins, two of which do not go directly to the liver thereby delaying the metabolism of THC to the more euphorogenic 11 hydroxy THC.

Another option is juicing. That is because the raw plant has cannabinoids in the acid form. THCa is not euphorogenic that is because the carboxy group effects the way the molecules fits into the CB1 receptor.

Other strategies include increasing CBD. CBD partially blocks the dysphoria caused by THC. It usually decreases it by one-third.

Another option is to try various terpenes. You can try caryophylin, a terpene found in pepper. A trick used by recreational consumers who have dysphoria is to bite down on a peppercorn (caryophylin is found in pepper). There is anecdotal evidence that combining pine nuts with a citrus fruit (a combination of pinene and limonene) can provide relief for patients who have ingested more than the preferred amount of THC.

Anxiety:	whole plant extract containing 2.5-5 mg 1:1 THC (CBD)
Nausea:	2.5-5 mg dronabinol or a similar dose of THC contained in a whole plant extract.
Insomnia:	5-10 mg THC from a whole plant vaporized or smoked to go to sleep,5-10 mg. of THC (dronabinol) or edible at bedtime for stay asleep.. May add 5-15 mg.CBD.
Pain:	15-30 mg or more of THC with a similar amount of CBD. CBD decreases possible dysphoria and is also useful in cases of inflammation contributing to the pain.
Autism Spectrum Disorder:	This varies enormously, from 2.5-5 mg of THC two-three times a day to as much as 25 mg of CBD alone. But, there is wide variability in THC and CBD dose and THC:CBD ratio. I had one case that showed dramatic results with 25 mg of CBD. It is not clear what THC:CBD ratio is best, although there is a study currently being conducted in Israel looking at the effects of a 20:1 CBD to THC ratio in the treatment of autism. This study is ongoing and has not yet been concluded.
Seizures:	While whole plant high CBD extract is popular, as is CBD alone, there is compelling research and historical evidence that THC plays an important role in controlling epilepsy. Relatively low doses of whole plant cannabis as infrequently as once a day have proven effective in decreasing seizure frequency; however, a somewhat higher dose may be necessary.
Cancer:	Dr. Donald Abrams, an oncologist at UCSF School of Medicine, has said that there is more than enough basic science evidence and anecdotal reports to justify doing a double-blind study. One such study was recently completed in the United Kingdom using 25 mg THC, 25 mg CBD. on glioblastoma patients. The treated groups had a 40% increase in survival time.[60] Lay healers may use 2-6x that dose.

Other Studies

The following are some examples of various studies done using dronabinol that show the variability of a "standard"

---

[60] Donald Abrams, M.D., "Marijuana for Medical Professionals Presentation," Denver, 2017.

dose. These studies are consistent with Unimed's (now Abbott's) position that a standard dose of dronabinol ranges from **2.5 up to 15 mg/sq. meter of body surface, taken 4-6x/day.**

- **Spasticity:** The late Dr. J. Thomas Ungerleider of UCLA led a study on the effects of cannabis on spasticity using doses of 2.5-15 mg of THC. He found that a dose of over 7.5 mg showed significant improvement in spasticity. Ungerleider et al. demonstrated clear dose-related reduction of spasticity with 7.5 to 15 mg THC.[61] Another study found that 10 mg THC reduced spasticity.[62] Also, GW Pharmaceuticals in England has had very good results in the treatment of the spasticity and pain related to multiple sclerosis with nabiximols. In speaking to their U.S. legal counsel Alice Mead, formally of the California Medical Association (CMA), the doses being used in these trials is or at least was proprietary information.[63]

- **Seizures:** In a double-blind clinical trial of CBD, Cunha et al. found it to be effective in abolishing or reducing seizures in seven out of eight subjects each receiving 100 mg daily, whereas only one out of seven placebo controls reported any improvement. The conclusion was that CBD had a beneficial effect in patients suffering from secondary generalized epilepsy who did not benefit from known antiepileptic drugs.[64]

---

[61] Ungerleider, J. Thomas, Therese Andyrsiak, Lynn Fairbanks, George W. Ellison, and Lawrence W. Myers. "Delta-9-THC in the treatment of spasticity associated with multiple sclerosis." *Advances in Alcohol & Substance Abuse* 7, no. 1 (1988): 39-50.

[62] Petro, Denis J., and C. Ellenberger. "Treatment of Human Spasticity with ?9-Tetrahydrocannabinol." *The Journal of Clinical Pharmacology* 21, no. S1 (1981).

[63] Novotna, A., J. Mares, S. Ratcliffe, I. Novakova, M. Vachova, O. Zapletalova, C. Gasperini et al. "A randomized, double-blind, placebo-controlled, parallel-group, enriched-design study of nabiximols (Sativex®), as add-on therapy, in subjects with refractory spasticity caused by multiple sclerosis." *European Journal of Neurology* 18, no. 9 (2011): 1122-1131.

[64] Cunha, Jomar M., E. A. Carlini, Aparecido E. Pereira, Oswaldo L. Ramos, Camilo Pimentel, Rubens Gagliardi, W. L. Sanvito, N. Lander, and R. Mechoulam. "Chronic administration of cannabidiol to healthy volunteers and epileptic patients." *Pharmacology* 21, no. 3 (1980): 175-185.

CHAPTER 10
ROUTES OF ADMINISTRATION

Different routes of cannabinoid administration have different effects. A full-spectrum hemp/cannabis oil supplement provides much more than simply THC and CBD. A whole plant tincture contains over 500 compounds including cannabinoids, minerals, fatty acids, flavonoids, and terpenes. If heat has been used in processing, some of the terpenes may have been destroyed.

Inhaled THC enters capillaries in the lungs, passes into general circulation through the pulmonary veins, and quickly crosses the blood-brain barrier. Without going through the liver it goes to the brain. When ingested orally, however, THC is absorbed in the small intestine and then carried to the liver, where it is metabolized by subclasses of Cytochrome P450 (abbreviated CYP), specifically the CYP2C and CYP3A enzymes. About 85% of the THC is metabolized to 11-hydroxy-THC which is more intoxicating than THC.

- **Smoking:** Most efficient and quickest acting but irritates the bronchial tree.
- **Vaporizing:** 70% fewer irritants than smoking and preserves more cannabinoids
- **Water Pipe (Bong):** Removes irritants and THC in equal proportions, cools smoke.
- **Sublingual:** Tinctures applied under the tongue act in about 15 minutes.
- **Tea:** Traditional form consumed for millennia in India. Can be made from leaves, roots, or flowering

tops. Usually made with milk or cream to absorb fat soluble cannabinoids.

- **Oral/Edibles:** Take 45 to 75 minutes to act. Read the label.
- **Topical:** Used for over a century by curanderos in Southern Mexico and Central America to treat arthritis in hands and wrists.
- **Prescription:** Dronabinol (Marinol) (THC), nabiximols (Sativex) (Canada, UK, NZ and EU), Cannabidiol (Epidiolex) - recently approved for sale in the US.
- **Rectal:** Full Extract Cannabis Oil suppositories can be used to decrease dysphoria .
- **Juicing:** The raw, newly picked plant (undried) has all its cannabinoids in the acid form including THCa (the non-psychotropic precursor to THC), CBDa, etc. There are usually limited or no euphorigenic effects from juicing a freshly picked cannabis plant.

Oral Ingestion

This is one of the oldest routes of administration, having been used in India as bhang tea since at least 1100 B.C.E. The drink must contain a fat such as dairy to capture the fat-soluble (lipophilic) molecules in cannabis. Of course, oral tinctures are widely used such as in prescription nabiximols and in flavored drinks to which cannabis has been added. This longer length of action with oral ingestion is helpful in the case of treating chronic conditions like Crohn's Disease or rheumatoid arthritis, but it can be disconcerting if the ingested dose is too high and leads to dysphoria.

As time goes on, this problem of consuming an unknown dose of THC is becoming less common because more and more edibles have the dose on their label and the majority of cannabis consumers understand what an appropriate dose is for them. Furthermore, we are seeing an increase in therapeutic use of high CBD and low THC containing products.

A Standardized Cannabis Medicine: Nabiximols

GW Pharmaceuticals has dealt with the issue of standardization and reproducible therapeutic results by creating a whole plant, alcohol extraction, tincture of cannabis product, Sativex™ (nabiximols). Sativex is produced through a proprietary recipe using standardized monocropped (cloned) plants. The company initially had six greenhouses in an old munitions factory in the south of England. Each greenhouse in use by GW is home to a different variety of cannabis and contains 10,000 plants. This growing process ensures consistency of plant material suitable for standardized pharmaceutical products.

The prescription pharmaceutical product nabiximols is made from the flowering tops of multiple plants thus further standardizing the product. It is composed of a 50/50 combination of two strains of cannabis; one high in THC and the other high in CBD. Nabiximols is a liquid, which is administered sublingually by a metered dose inhaler. In 2014, GW introduced Epidiolex™, a high CBD low THC, whole plant extract for treatment of epileptic seizures.[65]

Extensive studies have been done by GW Pharmaceuticals showing that their tincture of cannabis is much less psychotropic than dronabinol, which is a THC-only product.[66] Nabiximols is legal to prescribe in 24 countries, but the United States is not yet one of them despite successful phase III clinical trials for treatment of intractable pain completed in upstate New York in 2011. Epidiolex (cannabidiol) was approved in June 2018.

Marinol™ (Dronabinol) / Syndros™

In 1985 the federal government approved the sale of synthetic

[65] "History and Approach." GW Pharmaceuticals. Last modified 2016. https://www.gwpharm.com/about-us/history-approach/.

[66] Robson, Philip. "Abuse potential and psychoactive effects of d-9-tetrahydrocannabinol and cannabidiol oromucosal spray (Sativex), a new cannabinoid medicine." *Expert Opinion on Drug Safety* 10, no. 5 (2011): 675-685.

Marinol FDA Insert

HIGHLIGHTS OF PRESCRIBING INFORMATION These highlights do not include all of the information needed to use MARINOL® safely and effectively. See full prescribing information for MARINOL. MARINOL (dronabinol) capsules, for oral use, CIII Initial U.S. Approval: 1985 INDICATIONS AND USAGE MARINOL is a cannabinoid indicated in adults for the treatment of: • Anorexia associated with weight loss in patients with AIDS. (1) • Nausea and vomiting associated with cancer chemotherapy in patients who have failed to respond adequately to conventional antiemetic treatments. (1) DOSAGE AND ADMINISTRATION Anorexia Associated with Weight Loss in Adult Patients with AIDS (2.1): • The recommended adult starting dosage is 2.5 mg orally twice daily, one hour before lunch and dinner. v See the full prescribing information for dosage titration to manage adverse reactions and to achieve desired therapeutic effect. Nausea and Vomiting Associated with Chemotherapy in Adult Patients Who Failed Conventional Antiemetics (2.2): • The recommended starting dosage is 5 mg/m2 , administered 1 to 3 hours prior to the administration of chemotherapy, then every 2 to 4 hours after chemotherapy, for a total of 4 to 6 doses per day. Administer the first dose on an empty stomach at least 30 minutes prior to eating; subsequent doses can be taken without regard to meals. • See the full prescribing information for dosage titration to manage adverse reactions and to achieve desired therapeutic effect. DOSAGE FORMS AND STRENGTHS • Capsules: 2.5 mg, 5 mg, 10 mg (3) CONTRAINDICATIONS • History of a hypersensitivity reaction to dronabinol or sesame oil (4) WARNINGS AND PRECAUTIONS • Neuropsychiatric Adverse Reactions: May cause psychiatric and cognitive effects and impair mental and/or physical abilities. Avoid use in patients with a psychiatric history. Monitor for symptoms and avoid concomitant use of drugs with similar effects. Inform patients not to operate motor vehicles or other dangerous machinery until they are reasonably certain that MARINOL does not affect them adversely. (5.1) • Hemodynamic Instability: Patients with cardiac disorders may experience hypotension, hypertension, syncope or tachycardia. Avoid concomitant use of drugs with similar effects and monitor for hemodynamic changes after initiating or increasing the dosage of MARINOL. (5.2) o Seizures and Seizure-like Activity: Weigh the potential risk versus benefits before prescribing MARINOL to patients with a history of seizures, including those requiring anti-epileptic medication or with other factors that lower the seizure threshold. Monitor patients and discontinue if seizures occur. (5.3) • Multiple Substance Abuse: Assess risk for abuse or misuse in patients with a history of substance abuse or dependence, prior to prescribing MARINOL and monitor for the development of associated behaviors or conditions. (5.4) • Paradoxical Nausea, Vomiting, or Abdominal Pain: Consider dose reduction or discontinuation, if worsening of symptoms while on treatment. (5.5) ADVERSE REACTIONS • Most common adverse reactions (=3%) are: abdominal pain, dizziness, euphoria, nausea, paranoid reaction, somnolence, thinking abnormal and vomiting. (6.1) To report SUSPECTED ADVERSE REACTIONS, contact AbbVie Inc. at 1-800-633-9110 or FDA at 1-800-FDA-1088 or www.fda.gov/medwatch. DRUG INTERACTIONS o Inhibitors and inducers of CYP2C9 and CYP3A4: May alter dronabinol systemic exposure; monitor for potential dronabinol-related adverse reactions or loss of efficacy. (7.3) • Highly protein-bound drugs: Potential for displacement of other drugs from plasma proteins; monitor for adverse reactions to concomitant highly protein-bound drugs and narrow therapeutic index drugs (e.g., warfarin, cyclosporine, amphotericin B) when initiating or increasing the dosage of MARINOL. (7.4) USE IN SPECIFIC POPULATIONS • Pregnancy: May cause fetal harm. (8.1) • Lactation: Advise HIV-infected women not to breastfeed. Advise women with nausea and vomiting associated with cancer chemotherapy not to breastfeed during treatment with MARINOL and for 9 days after the last dose. (8.2) • Geriatric Use: Elderly patients may be more sensitive to the neuropsychiatric and postural hypotensive effects. Consider a lower starting dose in elderly patients. (2.1, 2.2, 5.1, 5.2, 8.5) See 17 for PATIENT COUNSELING INFORMATION and FDA-approved patient labeling. Revised: 08/2017

$\triangle$-9-THC capsules, generic name dronabinol, trade name Marinol™. It comes in 2.5, 5 and 10 mg doses. After oral administration, dronabinol (synthetic THC) has an onset of action of approximately 30 minutes to one hour and peak effect at 2-4 hours. Duration of action for psychoactive effects is 4 to 6 hours, but the appetite stimulant effect of dronabinol may continue for 24 hours or longer after administration. A recently approved variation is Syndros™, which is dronabinol in variable-doses delivered via a needleless syringe for ingestion.

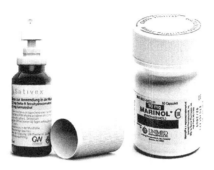

Marinol/Syndros (Dronabinol) vs. Sativex (Nabiximols)

Why is nabiximols less of a euphoriant than dronabinol? There are at least two reasons:

1) Nabiximols is liquid cannabis (a mixture of two whole plant alcohol extracts) and therefore the entourage effect is present. The presence of over 100 cannabinoids, particularly CBD, and over 200 terpenes makes it more effective than dronabinol and with fewer side effects.

2) Dronabinol contains only THC, the principle euphoriant in cannabis, and no CBD. This means dronabinol is more likely to cause dysphoria than cannabis. There are no other cannabinoids present in dronabinol, eliminating the possibility of engaging the entourage effect. There is no CBD present to block out the intoxicating effect of THC.

Dronabinol Intoxication/Euphoria

Most patients tolerate 2.5 to 5 mg doses of dronabinol (THC) with little or no euphoria, but at 10 mg, a small percentage of patients will begin to dislike the way they feel. The percentage of patients with complaints of dysphoria increases at 15 mg.

To manage this side effect, use whole plant cannabis which contains an equal or greater amount of CBD.

While CBD partially blocks THC euphoria, the euphoria can still occur. I had one patient who took a product with 30 mg each of THC and CBD and he complained of altered states. From that experience my guess is that CBD blocks about 25-40% of THC induced euphoria. The best advice as a general guide for cannabis dosing is to start low (particularly with the dose of THC) and go slow when increasing.

Side Effects of Dronabinol

The Physician's Desk Reference (PDR) is hundreds of pages long and contains the side effects and warnings for most of today's manufactured prescription drugs. These synthetically manufactured medications often have greater side effects than plant-based medicines. There are several negative side effects experienced by patients who consume dronabinol.

Dronabinol contains only THC. It is without the other cannabinoids and terpenes, particularly CBD, which would balance and control THC's euphorigenic effects. Dronabinol is more expensive, has more side effects, and doesn't work as well as cannabis. Some of dronabinol's adverse effects include: dizziness, drowsiness, hyperemesis, nausea, and seizures. To be fair, it does have considerable off-label effectiveness and there are several reasons to prescribe it.

Rescheduling of THC

Attesting to the safety of cannabis is the FDA's rescheduling of synthetic THC (dronabinol). The FDA rarely moves a drug to a lower schedule. In the case of THC, the most psychoactive constituent of cannabis, dronabinol was moved in 1999 from schedule II to schedule III, where it remains to this day. Interestingly, botanical cannabis has fewer side effects than the synthetic product, dronabinol, despite the schedule classification suggesting otherwise.

Juicing

Juicing the raw leaves and consuming the juice doesn't produce a "high" because all the cannabinoids in the raw plant are in the acid form (have a carboxyl group). There are trace levels of THC in fresh cannabis, but THCa is the dominant cannabinoid, which is non-psychotropic. For THCa to cause a "high" it needs to be decarboxylated into THC. This decarboxylation occurs by drying over several days or heating. Juicing raw cannabis takes advantage of THCa and therefore allows use of high doses of cannabinoid acids. When eaten, vaporized, or smoked, higher doses of decarboxylated cannabis can often cause unpleasant euphoria. Higher doses are required for use of cannabis as an anti-proliferative agent.

https://www.projectcbd.org/about/cannabis-facts/juicing-raw-cannabis

William Courtney, M.D. is the world's leading juicing proponent. He recommends that his patients mix the cannabis juice (1 part) with carrot juice (10 parts) to counteract the bitterness and drink the mixture three times a day. Dr. Courtney suggests that the cannabis plant has the highest CBD at 70-90 days after sowing. After 90 days they rapidly produce

more THC.[67] Potential conditions that may benefit from raw
cannabis include autoimmune disorders, inflammatory
disorders, and possibly various types of cancer or pre-cancer
dysplasias.

Respiratory

- **Smoking**

  As noted under side effects, the smoking of cannabis
  is associated with increased cough, sputum
  production and bronchial irritation, but
  conspicuously not cancer. The benefits of the
  respiratory route are the rapid onset and the ability to
  titrate the dosage. Migraines, social anxiety, nausea,
  seizures, and asthma are conditions where rapid
  onset is beneficial.

- **Vaporizing**

  This method heats cannabis to a vaporization point
  but below the point of combustion. Vaporization
  therefore does not burn the plant material, but rather
  releases the volatile oils into the air. This results in
  roughly 70% less irritation to the bronchial tree than
  smoking. This process still provides rapid onset and
  the ability to titrate dosage. There are both individual
  vaporizers, like e-cigarettes, as well as less portable
  table vaporizers such as the Volcano.

- **Water Pipe (Bong)**

  This is a device that uses water to cool and filter the
  cannabis smoke. It not only filters out bronchial
  irritants but filters out THC and other plant
  constituents in the same proportion. The water traps
  a percentage of the toxins, carcinogens and products
  of pyrolysis.

Topical

Topical application of cannabis salves is useful for relief of
arthritic pain close to the body's surface, such as in the fingers

---

[67] "The Importance of THC free Cannabis." Cannabis Digest.
https://cannabisdigest.ca/importance-thc-free-cannabis/.

or wrists. Topical application can also promote the relief of muscle spasms, particularly in the trapezius. It also can be helpful in treating numerous skin conditions. Using topical applications does not produce a psychotropic effect. Topical application of tinctures of cannabis has been used for arthritis pain relief for over 100 years by Curanderos, lay healers, in Southern Mexico and Central America.

CHAPTER 11
METABOLISM

Cannabis and cannabinoids are metabolized by the cytochrome P450 (CYP) enzyme system.[68] The CYP system contributes to the metabolism of drugs by oxidizing them. This generally means incorporating an oxygen atom into the drug's molecular structure. Oxidation will usually make a compound more water-soluble and therefore easier for the kidneys to filter out.

CBD and other plant cannabinoids have the potential to inhibit or increase the plasma levels of many pharmaceuticals by inhibiting or activating the activity of the CYP enzymes.[67] This enzyme group metabolizes most of the drugs we consume. In sufficient dosage CBD can temporarily deactivate CYP enzymes.[69] This alters the metabolism of many compounds including THC.

Certain compounds in grapefruit can inhibit the expression of some cytochrome P450 enzymes. CBD is a more potent inhibitor of CYP enzymes than the grapefruit compound bergapten (the strongest of several grapefruit components that inhibit CYPs, also known to give Bergamot tea its distinctive smell and flavor).[70]

CBD reduces the enzymatic degradation of Warfarin, thereby increasing its duration of action and effect. A person taking a CBD-rich product should seek the advice of their

---

[68] Watanabe, Kazuhito, Satoshi Yamaori, Tatsuya Funahashi, Toshiyuki Kimura, and Ikuo Yamamoto. "Cytochrome P450 enzymes involved in the metabolism of tetrahydrocannabinols and cannabinol by human hepatic microsomes." *Life Sciences* 80, no. 15 (2007): 1415-1419

[69] Stout, Stephen M., and Nina M. Cimino. "Exogenous cannabinoids as substrates, inhibitors, and inducers of human drug metabolizing enzymes: a systematic review." *Drug Metabolism Reviews* 46, no. 1 (2014): 86-95.

[70] Jiang, Rongrong, Satoshi Yamaori, Shuso Takeda, Ikuo Yamamoto, and Kazuhito Watanabe. "Identification of cytochrome P450 enzymes responsible for metabolism of cannabidiol by human liver microsomes." *Life Sciences* 89, no. 5-6 (2011): 165-170.

physician. If the patient is taking Coumadin checking clotting time and adjusting dosage accordingly is necessary. Conversely, as a physician you might check blood levels of Warfarin and adjust dosage.

Half-Life / Length of Effect

Because it is fat soluble, when THC enters the bloodstream it is rapidly absorbed by adipose tissue (half-life: 30 minutes). On its first pass through the liver, 85% of THC is metabolized to 11-hydroxy-THC (11-OH-THC). This metabolite contributes significantly to the psychotropic effects of cannabis. It activates the CB1 cannabinoid receptor in the brain and produces euphoria greater than the parent compound, $\triangle$-9-THC.

After having absorbed into the body fat, the THC then gradually returns to the bloodstream, where it goes to the liver, is metabolized, and is eliminated in urine and feces (half-life: a few days!). With repeated use THC tends to accumulate in adipose tissue and the liver. THC itself has been found in blood toxicology screens up to a week after last use in a regular user. After a week, THC is still in the blood but falls below the detection level and a metabolic 9-carboxy-THC is concentrated in the urine. As a result, in regular consumers of cannabis, THC metabolites can still be found in the urine weeks after last use.

Onset of Effects

When smoked, the acute effects of cannabis begin within a few minutes. The plasma concentration peaks after seven to 10 minutes, but the peak effect is usually felt after 20 to 30 minutes. Some effects may last for two to three hours. When consumed orally, cannabis takes effect one to two hours after consumption, and the therapeutic effects, as well as "the high", can last from three to eight hours.

CHAPTER 12
MEDICINAL USES OF CANNABIS

Therapeutic Applications of Cannabis

ADD/ADHD treatment
Antibacterial
Anti-nauseant/Anti-emetic
Analgesic
Anti-epileptic
Anti-inflammatory
Anxiolytic
Anti-depressant
Anti-spasmodic
Appetite stimulant
Bronchodilator
Encourages apoptosis
Inhibiting angiogenesis
Inhibits cancer growth
Inhibits Id-1 Gene
PTSD treatment
Reduces blood sugar levels
Sleep Aid
Stimulation of bone growth
Vasorelaxation

Conditions Cannabis May Help

Analgesia

Intractable pain
Neuropathic pain

Osteoarthritis
Other forms of chronic pain
Phantom limb pain

Autoimmune Diseases

Crohn's Disease
Complex Regional Pain Syndrome
Fibromyalgia
Lupus Erythematosus
Reflex Sympathetic Dystrophy
Rheumatoid Arthritis
Scleroderma

Endocannabinoid Deficiency Syndrome

Attention Deficit Disorder (ADD) and Attention
    Deficit Hyperactivity Disorder (ADHD)
Autism Spectrum Disorder (ASD)
    Autism
Asperger's syndrome
Social anxiety
OCD
Bipolar disorder
Crohn's Disease
Explosive disorder
Obsessive Compulsive Disorder (OCD)
Panic attacks
Tourette's Syndrome

Gastrointestinal

Anorexia
Appetite Stimulation
Irritable bowel disease, ulcerative colitis and
    Crohn's Disease
Nausea

Mental Health

ADD
Anger management issues

Anxiety
Bipolar disorder
Depression
Hypervigilant syndrome
Impulse control issues
Mood disorders
OCD
Panic attacks
PTSD
Stress relief

Motor Control

Dystonia
Essential tremor
Multiple Sclerosis
Parkinson's disease
Tourette's syndrome

Neurodegenerative Disease / Neurodegeneration (see also: Motor Control)

Alzheimer's Disease
Amyotrophic Lateral Sclerosis (ALS) (Lou Gehrig's Disease)
Cerebellar degeneration
Huntington's Disease
Multiple Sclerosis (MS)
Parkinson's Disease

Other/General

Addiction/Harm Reduction Substitute
AIDS - pain/appetite
Asthma
Cancer
Epilepsy and Seizures
Glaucoma
Insomnia and other sleep disorders
Migraine

Motion Sickness
Neuroprotective
PTSD
Relief of pain
Skin Conditions
Spinal Cord Injury
Stroke and TBI

Analgesia

Several constituents of cannabis contribute to its analgesic effects, not just THC and CBD. These constituents include CBN, CBG and several terpenes. Cannabinoids can decrease the frequency of pain signals through retrograde inhibition. By slowing the speed of neurotransmission, the brain is receiving fewer pain signals. An increase in cannabinoids also causes the cannabinoid modulated central pain interpretation center (one of two such pain centers-the other one is mediated by the endorphins) to interpret pain as less severe. Many patients say that they have less pain, and some say they still have the pain, but it is easier to concentrate on something else, while others say that it is a combination of the two.

Cannabis-Like Substances in Brain Relieve Pain

As long ago as 1999, a report on the proceedings of the National Academy of Sciences, *Marijuana as Medicine: Assessing the Science Base*, stated, "U.S. researchers report that pain triggers the release of a marijuana-like chemical called anandamide *(Note: Anandamide is an endogenous cannabinoid neurotransmitter)* deep in the brain that works as a natural pain reliever. Anandamide levels in the brain also rose significantly in response to painful stimuli.[71]

"The fall in pain perception was paralleled by a significant rise in the levels of anandamide in a portion of the brain called the periaqueductal gray, or PAG. The increase of anandamide in the PAG resulted in greatly diminished pain sensitivity in

[71] Joy, Janet, Stanley J. Watson, Jr., and John A. Benson, eds. *Marijuana and Medicine: Assessing the Science Base* Washington D.C.: National Academy Press, 1999

the rat. The rats' pain perception returned to normal after being administered a substance that blocked anandamide."[72]

This study supports a second endocannabinoid-mediated pain interpretation center in the brain, other than that mediated by endorphins. The report also hypothesizes that these results, when taken together, support the existence of a pain control system within the periaqueductal gray region (PAG). The report goes on to state that this pain control center, "...is triggered by pain and promotes analgesia through the release of anandamide." Consistent with these findings, the researchers suggest that drugs that affect the endocannabinoid system might form the basis of a modern approach to the treatment of pain. And, in fact, a study of 300 patient charts done by the American Academy of Cannabinoid Medicine (AACM) revealed pain relief to be the number one reason for cannabinoid medicine specialists recommending medicinal use of cannabis.

Neurodegenerative Disease

Even more important than providing some relief for symptoms of TBIs, cannabis and cannabinoids are neuroprotective; they can prevent neuronal cell death. A study published in the *Journal of Neuroscience* demonstrated that synthetic cannabinoids can succeed in preventing neurodegenerative processes. This is but one of many basic research studies which suggest that cannabinoids can treat inflammation in the brain and may protect humans from the cognitive decline associated with Alzheimer's disease.[73]

Neuroprotective

Cannabinoid medicine specialists frequently see patients who have suffered ischemic brain damage from stroke or traumatic

---

[72] Walker, J. Michael, Susan M. Huang, Nicole M. Strangman, Kang Tsou, and M. Clara Sañudo-Peña. "Pain modulation by release of the endogenous cannabinoid anandamide." *Proceedings of the National Academy of Sciences* 96, no. 21 (1999): 12198-12203
[73] Ramírez, Belén G., Cristina Blázquez, Teresa Gómez del Pulgar, Manuel Guzmán, and María L. de Ceballos. "Prevention of Alzheimer's disease pathology by cannabinoids: neuroprotection mediated by blockade of microglial activation." *Journal of Neuroscience* 25, no. 8 (2005): 1904-1913.

brain injury (TBI) that benefit from the medicinal use of cannabis. Cannabis can address their symptoms of anxiety, depression, tremors and explosive anger.

CBD reduces neuroinflammation and promotes neuro-plasticity (the ability of neurons to adapt and provide a function they were not originally designed for) and functional recovery after brain ischemia.

A synthetic cannabinoid, dexabinol, has been shown to treat neuro-inflammatory disorders and preserve neural function. In

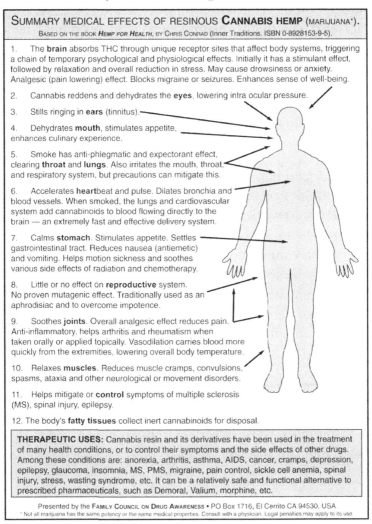

SUMMARY MEDICAL EFFECTS OF RESINOUS **CANNABIS HEMP** (MARIJUANA*).
BASED ON THE BOOK *HEMP FOR HEALTH*, BY CHRIS CONRAD (Inner Traditions. ISBN 0-8928153-9-5).

1.   The **brain** absorbs THC through unique receptor sites that affect body systems, triggering a chain of temporary psychological and physiological effects. Initially it has a stimulant effect, followed by relaxation and overall reduction in stress. May cause drowsiness or anxiety. Analgesic (pain lowering) effect. Blocks migraine or seizures. Enhances sense of well-being.

2.   Cannabis reddens and dehydrates the **eyes**, lowering intra ocular pressure.

3.   Stills ringing in **ears** (tinnitus).

4.   Dehydrates **mouth**, stimulates appetite, enhances culinary experience.

5.   Smoke has anti-phlegmatic and expectorant effect, clearing **throat** and **lungs**. Also irritates the mouth, throat, and respiratory system, but precautions can mitigate this.

6.   Accelerates **heart**beat and pulse. Dilates bronchia and blood vessels. When smoked, the lungs and cardiovascular system add cannabinoids to blood flowing directly to the brain — an extremely fast and effective delivery system.

7.   Calms **stomach**. Stimulates appetite. Settles gastrointestinal tract. Reduces nausea (antiemetic) and vomiting. Helps motion sickness and soothes various side effects of radiation and chemotherapy.

8.   Little or no effect on **reproductive** system. No proven mutagenic effect. Traditionally used as an aphrodisiac and to overcome impotence.

9.   Soothes **joints**. Overall analgesic effect reduces pain. Anti-inflammatory, helps arthritis and rheumatism when taken orally or applied topically. Vasodilation carries blood more quickly from the extremities, lowering overall body temperature.

10.   Relaxes **muscles**. Reduces muscle cramps, convulsions, spasms, ataxia and other neurological or movement disorders.

11.   Helps mitigate or **control** symptoms of multiple sclerosis (MS), spinal injury, epilepsy.

12. The body's **fatty tissues** collect inert cannabinoids for disposal.

THERAPEUTIC USES: Cannabis resin and its derivatives have been used in the treatment of many health conditions, or to control their symptoms and the side effects of other drugs. Among these conditions are: anorexia, arthritis, asthma, AIDS, cancer, cramps, depression, epilepsy, glaucoma, insomnia, MS, PMS, migraine, pain control, sickle cell anemia, spinal injury, stress, wasting syndrome, etc. It can be a relatively safe and functional alternative to prescribed pharmaceuticals, such as Demoral, Valium, morphine, etc.

Presented by the FAMILY COUNCIL ON DRUG AWARENESS • PO Box 1716, El Cerrito CA 94530, USA
* Not all marijuana has the same potency or the same medical properties. Consult with a physician. Legal penalties may apply to its use.

studies comparing a placebo control group to patients that had been placed on a heart-lung bypass machine as part of cardiac bypass surgery, the dexabinol treated patients performed better post-operatively on a series of tests designed to check mental acuity. This is important because being on a bypass machine is known to decrease mental acuity, at least temporarily, in over 40% of bypass patients.[74]

A 2017 study conducted in Brazil investigated the effects of CBD on the cognitive and emotional impairments induced by bilateral common carotid artery occlusion (BCCAO) in mice. CBD also stimulated neurogenesis and promoted dendritic restructuring in the hippocampus of BCCAO animals.[75] Collectively, the results demonstrate that short-term CBD treatment results in global functional recovery in ischemic mice and impacts multiple and distinct targets involved in the pathophysiology of brain ischemic injury.

Stroke

The endocannabinoids, anandamide (aka N-arachidonyl ethanolamide) or AEA, and 2-arachidonoylglycerol, (2-AG) are believed to work in four ways to reduce brain damage from ischemia:

- First, cannabinoids reduce the levels of glutamate, a toxic molecule, released after injury
- Second and third, they decrease free radicals and tumor necrosis factor (TNF) a chemical that induces inflammation after injury
- Fourth, 2-AG increases the blood supply to the brain. All four mechanisms contribute to limiting the cellular damage done after the primary insult to the brain from blood loss and decreased oxygen.

Examining CBD's effect on mitochondria sheds light on how CBD can protect against brain injury by regulating

---

[74] Ibid.

[75] Mori, Marco Aurélio, Erika Meyer, Ligia Mendes Soares, Humberto Milani, Francisco Silveira Guimarães, and Rúbia Maria Weffort de Oliveira. "Cannabidiol reduces neuroinflammation and promotes neuroplasticity and functional recovery after brain ischemia." *Progress in Neuro-Psychopharmacology and Biological Psychiatry* 75 (2017): 94-105.

fluctuations in intracellular calcium. A November 2016 study in the *European Journal of Pharmacology* found that an "imbalance of sodium and calcium homeostasis trigger[s] pathophysiological processes in cerebral ischemia, which accelerate[s] neuronal brain death."[76] According to Iranian scientists at Shahid Beheshti University in Tehran, the good news for stroke victims is that CBD can reduce the severity of ischemic damage by enhancing NCX receptor expression on the mitochondrial membrane.[77]

Exit Drug—Harm Reduction Substitute

There is a growing body of clinical evidence that cannabis can be used to help counter drug dependencies sometimes referred to as addictions. Diana Cichewicz at Virginia Commonwealth University has shown that THC blocks the development of tolerance and withdrawal in experimental animals.[78] Clinicians in 19th century America and Europe knew the same thing.

Many cannabinoid medical specialists have patients where cannabis has proven to be a useful harm reduction substitute for alcohol, opiates, cocaine, and tobacco, in that order. The study by AACM of 300 patients, 100 each from three different cannabinoid medicine specialists revealed that about 1-2% of patients were using cannabis for harm reduction.[79]

Cancer: Encourage Apoptosis/Decrease Stress

Endocannabinoids can create a positive feedback loop, increasing stress to the point where the cell undergoes apoptosis (planned cell death). Plant cannabinoids can also induce apoptosis under similar conditions. The death of

---

[76] Khaksar, Sepideh, and Mohammad Reza Bigdeli. "Anti-excitotoxic effects of cannabidiol are partly mediated by enhancement of NCX2 and NCX3 expression in animal model of cerebral ischemia." *European Journal of Pharmacology* 794 (2017): 270-279.

[77] Ibid.

[78] Cichewicz, Diana L., and Sandra P. Welch. "Modulation of oral morphine antinociceptive tolerance and naloxone-precipitated withdrawal signs by oral △-9-tetrahydrocannabinol." *Journal of Pharmacology and Experimental Therapeutics* 305, no. 3 (2003): 812-817.

[79] Judson, Kim, PhD and David Bearman MD. Demographic Study, 2016. Publication Pending

cancer cells promotes homeostasis and the survival of the organism as a whole.

Recently, researchers in Great Britain found that in vivo cancer cells contain cannabinoid receptors on the surface of the cell wall. The introduction of exogenous cannabinoids to cancer cells induces apoptosis (cell death) of the cancer cell only. The presence of cannabinoids also prohibits the production of AGF (andgiogenic growth factor) from cancer cells. This growth factor is utilized by cancer cells to develop their own blood supply. It is a reasonable assumption to conclude that without a blood supply, cancer cells cannot proliferate.[80]

Researchers in Israel have also conducted research regarding cannabis' effectiveness in cancer inhibition. These same researchers have also provided evidence of the effectiveness of cannabis for osteoporosis prevention.[81]

A report by British researchers in the *Journal of Neuroscience* (2009) noted that "under pathological conditions involving mitochondrial dysfunction and calcium [Ca(2+)] dysregulation, CBD may prove beneficial in promoting apoptotic signaling via a restoration of calcium homeostasis.[82]

The ebb and flow of calcium and stress, autophagy and cell death, the restoration of homeostasis on a cellular level are regulated by CBD.

Cancer Chemoprevention and Therapy by Monoterpenes

Terpenes also play a role in preventing apoptosis. Researcher M.N. Gould describes this process as follows:

"Monoterpenes are found in the essential oils of many plants including fruits, vegetables, and herbs [and]

---

[80] Guzman, M.. Cannabinoids as Possible Antitumoral Drugs. Presented at the Tenth National Clinical Conference on Cannabis Therapeutics.; 2016; Baltimore,, MD.
[81] Somurn-Jaouni, R. Recent Advances. Presented at the Tenth National Clinical Conference on Cannabis Therapeutics.; 2016; Baltimore,, MD.
[82] Ryan, Duncan, Alison J. Drysdale, Carlos Lafourcade, Roger G. Pertwee, and Bettina Platt. "Cannabidiol targets mitochondria to regulate intracellular Ca2+ levels." *Journal of Neuroscience* 29, no. 7 (2009): 2053-20673.

prevent the carcinogenesis process at both the initiation and promotion/progression stages. In addition, monoterpenes are effective in treating early and advanced cancers. Monoterpenes such as limonene and perillyl alcohol have been shown to prevent mammary, liver, and other cancers. The monoterpenes inhibit the isoprenylation of small G-proteins. Such inhibitions could alter signal transduction and result in altered gene expression. These compounds have also been used to treat a variety of rodent cancers, including breast and pancreatic carcinomas. In addition, in vitro data suggest that they may be effective in treating neuroblastomas and leukemias. Both limonene and perillyl alcohol are currently being evaluated in phase I clinical trials in advanced cancer patients."[83]

Mechanism of Action

Researchers are still pondering the mechanisms by which cannabis promotes apoptosis. Here is one theory informed by the theories of biochemist Dennis Hill:

Every cell has a group of sphingolipids that manage the life and death of that cell. A profile of factors is called the "Sphingolipid Rheostat." If endogenous ceramide (a signaling metabolite of sphingosine-1-phosphate) is high, then cell death (apoptosis) is imminent. If ceramide is low, the cell is strong and vital.

THC causes an increase in ceramide synthesis. As Hill puts it, "when THC connects to the CB1 or CB2 cannabinoid receptor site on the cancer cell, it causes an increase in ceramide synthesis which drives cell death." He notes that "a normal healthy cell does not produce ceramide in the presence of THC, thus is not affected by the cannabinoid." Thus cancer cell death is not due to cell poisoning from the cytotoxic chemicals.

---

[83] Belville, Russ. "National Cancer Institute Scrubs 'Antitumoral Effect' of Cannabinoids From Website." HuffPost. April 8, 2011. http://www.huffingtonpost.com/russ-belville/national-cancer-institute_b_842631.html/.

According to Hill there is a very tiny shift in the mitochondria. Most cells contain a cell nucleus, hundreds to thousands of mitochondria, and various other organelles in the cytoplasm. The purpose of the mitochondria is to produce energy (ATP) for cell use. As ceramide starts to accumulate, turning up the Sphingolipid Rheostat, it increases the mitochondrial membrane pore permeability to cytochrome-c, a critical protein in energy synthesis. Cytochrome-c is pushed out of the mitochondria, killing the source of energy for the cell. As noted above, there is considerable research also demonstrating a role for terpenes in promoting cancer cell death.

National Cancer Institute

In a PDQ update from March 17, 2011, the National Cancer Institute addressed this relationship between cancer care and cannabis. This update was censored and removed only 11 days after its initial release. The Institute acknowledged, "The potential effects of medicinal cannabis for people living with cancer include antiemetic effects, appetite stimulation, pain relief, anti-anxiety and improved sleep. In the practice of integrative oncology, the health care provider may recommend medicinal cannabis not only for symptom management but also for its possible direct anti-tumor effect."[84]

The NCI followed this release with new government-supported information and a report that examined whether patients who smoke marijuana rather than ingesting it orally were exposed to a higher risk of lung and certain digestive system cancers." This "fake news" prompted a strong reaction from The Advocates for the Disabled and Seriously Ill (ADSI)."[85] According to the ADSI, the findings of 19 government studies resulted in a failure to "demonstrate statistically significant associations between marijuana inhalation and lung cancer." The report also identified a

---

[84] "Federal Government Reports Marijuana Effective in Combating Certain Cancers Reports ADSI." Globe Newswire. March 12, 2013. https://globenewswire.com/news-release/2013/03/12/530022/10024825/en/Federal-Government-Reports-Marijuana-Effective-in-Combatting-Certain-Cancers-Reports-ADSI.html
[85] Ibid.

separate study of 611 lung cancer patients that showed cannabis was "not associated with an increased risk of lung cancer or other upper aero digestive tract cancers and found no positive associations with any cancer type."[86] The ADSI further noted a study by Spanish researcher Dr. Manuel Guzman on dronabinol, in which patients with recurrent glioblastoma were given an intratumoral injection of $\triangle$-9-THC. The study resulted in tumor reduction in a number of test participants.[87]

The ADSI went on to report that "in addition to anti-cancer properties, separate research reported marijuana appears to have profound neuro-protective and brain-enhancing properties that could potentially treat many neurodegenerative disorders."[88] When it comes to glioblastoma, a recent study in England with nabiximols using 25 mg of THC and 25 mg of CBD whole plant alcohol extract three times a day, demonstrated that survival time after diagnosis increased by 40% in the study group over the control group (330 days to 510 days).[89]

More Modern Research on the Analgesic Properties of Cannabis

- **Institute of Medicine**

  There is a substantial body of anecdotal and research-based evidence of cannabis's analgesic properties. In 1982 the Institute of Medicine (IOM) reported that, "several animal models have been used to show analgesic effects of cannabis and its analogues." As examples they cited Grunfeld and Edery, 1969, Sofia et al., 1973, and Noyes et al, 1976. Each of these studies found a reduction in pain reports by cancer patients given oral $\triangle$-9-THC.[90]

---

[86] Ibid.

[87] Ibid.

[88] Ibid.

[89] Noyes, Russell, S. Fred Brunk, David H. Avery, and Arthur Canter. "Psychologic effects of oral delta-9-tetrahydrocannabinol in advanced cancer patients." *Comprehensive Psychiatry* (1976).

[90] GW Pharmaceuticals Achieves Positive Results in Phase 2 Proof of Concept Study in Glioma," GW Pharmaceuticals. https://www.gwpharm.com/about-us/news/gw-pharmaceuticals-achieves-positive-results-phase-2-proof-of-concept-study-glioma

The 1999 Institute of Medicine report on medical cannabis, *Marijuana and Medicine: Assessing the Science Base*, stated: "The accumulated data indicate a potential therapeutic value for cannabinoid drugs, particularly for symptoms such as pain relief, control of nausea and vomiting, and appetite stimulation."[91] They concluded that cannabis had medical value and that its side effects were similar to the bulk of prescription drugs then on the market.

- **Society for Neuroscience**

  In 1997, a *Los Angeles Times* article reported on several studies presented at the Society for Neuroscience addressing cannabis's painkilling properties. These studies were done at such institutions as University of Texas, University of Minnesota, Brown University, Wake Forest School of Medicine, and University of California at San Francisco (UCSF). According to the *Times* article, researchers reported that "active chemicals found in the plant could serve as an effective remedy for the millions who suffer serious pain each year without the unwanted side effects of more traditional morphine-like drugs."[92]

- **California Center for Medicinal Cannabis Research (CMCR)**

  The center located at University of California at San Diego (UCSD) School of Medicine coordinates and supports cannabis research throughout the state. Four diseases and/or conditions were designated as areas of emphasis for CMCR funding. One symptom was chronic pain, and particularly neuropathic pain. In 2011 the CMCR released a summary of the 18 FDA-approved clinically related studies completed at four UC medical schools. At least five of these

---

[91] Joy, Janet, Stanley J. Watson, Jr., and John A. Benson, eds. *Marijuana and Medicine: Assessing the Science Base.* Washington D.C.: National Academy Press, 1999.

[92] Chemicals in Pot Cut Severe Pain, Study Says." *Los Angeles Times.* Last Modified October 27, 1997.

studies had to do with relief of pain and at least two were published in peer-reviewed medical journals.

- **University of New Mexico**

  University of New Mexico researchers evaluated prescription drug use patterns over a 24-month period. They compared opiate use in 83 pain patients enrolled in the state's medical cannabis program to 42 non-enrolled patients. The study reported that 36% of the program registrants significantly reduced their prescription drug intake while non-registrants diagnosed with similar conditions did not.[88] Furthermore, by the study's end, 34% of registered cannabis program patients had eliminated their use of prescription drugs altogether.

  The authors wrote, "Legal access to cannabis may reduce the use of multiple classes of dangerous prescription medications in certain patient populations." They concluded, "[a] shift from prescriptions for other scheduled drugs to cannabis may result in less frequent interactions with our conventional healthcare system and potentially improved patient health."[93]

- **Cost Savings/Bradford Research**

  A study published in the journal Health Affairs reported that medical cannabis access is associated with lower Medicaid expenditures and Medicare Part D approved prescription medications.[94] Moreover, in 2017 Forbes reported on the findings by Ashley C. Bradford and W. David Braford who analyzed 2007-2014 data that demonstrates that if "all states had legalized medical marijuana in 2014,

---

[93] Stith, Sarah S., Jacob M. Vigil, Ian Marshall Adams, and Anthony P. Reeve. "Effects of Legal Access to Cannabis on Scheduled II-V Drug Prescriptions." *Journal of the American Medical Directors Association* 19, no. 1 (2018): 59-64

[94] "Study: Medical Marijuana Legalization Linked to Lower Medicaid Costs." NORML. April 27, 2017. http://norml.org/news/2017/04/27/study-medical-marijuana-legalization-linked-to-lower-medicaid-costs/

Medicaid could have saved $1 billion in spending on prescriptions."

- **National Institute on Drug Abuse (NIDA)**

Nora Volkow, M.D., director of NIDA, long-time skeptic of cannabis's medicinal properties, was the keynote speaker at the 2017 American Society of Addiction Medicine (ASAM) meeting. Dr. Volkow spoke on strategies for dealing with the so-called opiate epidemic. Her first bullet point was to tell the addictionologists present at the conference that when possible cannabis should be recommended for pain relief rather than prescribing an opiate.

CHAPTER 13
SIDE EFFECTS OF CANNABIS

PHYSICAL	PSYCHOLOGICAL
Abdominal Hyperemesis	Dysphoria
Cardiac Transient Tachycardia	Panic attacks
Changes in Blood Pressure	Paranoia
Dizziness	Impaired Driving
Hand-Eye Coordination Changes	
Mild cough with smoke or vapor	

As prescription drug advertisements remind us, all medicines produce side effects. Sometimes these side effects are physically unpleasant, and in some cases, side effects can even be fatal. Cannabis, too, has discomforting side effects, but these are primarily legal or psychological rather than physical. Psychological effects are often related to the public stigmas associated with the plant, whereas physical effects are minor. Dependency risk of cannabis, interestingly, is less than coffee.[95] In addition, many studies show there is no adverse effect on IQ.[96] Studies that purport to demonstrate this have been poorly designed and not controlled for other important variables such as home environment, parents' rearing skills, Traumatic Brain Injury (TBI), ADD, PTSD, and/or use of other drugs both licit and illicit. Here are some potential side effects from cannabis:

---

[95] Phillip J. Hilts, "Negative Addictiveness of Drugs," *New York Times*, Aug. 2, 1994.

[96] Jackson, Nicholas J., Joshua D. Isen, Rubin Khoddam, Daniel Irons, Catherine Tuvblad, William G. Iacono, Matt McGue, Adrian Raine, and Laura A. Baker. "Impact of adolescent marijuana use on intelligence: Results from two longitudinal twin studies." *Proceedings of the National Academy of Sciences* 113, no. 5 (2016): E500-E508.

Physical

Abdominal: hyperemesis.
Cardiac Transient Tachycardia
Dizziness
Drowsiness
Hand-eye coordination: ambiguous
Respiratory: None if taken orally or used topically. If vaporized, mild cough.

Blood Pressure (BP)

A 1999 Institute of Medicine (IOM) report addresses the research on the effect of cannabis on blood pressure (BP). The report found that it raises or lowers BP by 5 mm of mercury (mm Hg). Although the report says its effects are not significant, it should be noted that there are reports of orthostatic hypotension in medical cannabis consumers. This author has a few male patients in their fifties who experienced blood pressure levels dramatically lowered from previously high and abnormal levels with use of cannabis.

Psychological

May affect judgment
Impaired driving
Panic attacks (usually in naïve users)
Paranoia (can occur particularly with high levels of THC in the naïve cases)

While there are many beneficial psychological effects to cannabis, there are some psychological side effects which may occur. These include panic attacks (usually in naïve users). Paranoia which can occur, particularly with high levels of THC, in the naïve users. It also may affect judgment. It may cause dysphoria. When a person is high they recognize it and adjust their driving accordingly.

Dysphoria

Dysphoria is excessive unpleasant euphoria. Dysphoria is usually related to naïve users using too high a percentage of THC and too low a percentage of CBD. Dysphoria is more likely to occur with the oral route of administration, but dysphoria may occur with smoking. On the other hand, euphoria itself can be therapeutic. Dr. Donald Abrams, UCSF Medical School professor, oncologist and AIDS treatment researcher says, "In my patient population a little euphoria is a good thing."[97]

A late spring 2014 article by *New York Times* columnist Maureen Dowd is a good example of the adverse effect of a naïve user consuming a high dose THC product. It appears Dowd did not understand that cannabis, much like most medication consumed by the oral route of administration, takes 45-75 minutes to take effect. She was impatient. After taking two reasonable doses 15 minutes apart, she ate the whole thing. The June 20, 2014 issue of *The Week* put it this way, "Dowd ate too much of a weed-laced candy bar, which had no dosing instructions, and spent eight hours curled up in a paranoid, catatonic, hallucinatory state."[98]

This is not a surprise. Dowd obviously had not fully researched her subject; so rather than use the respiratory route of administration where she could have more easily self-titrated the dose she would consume, she orally consumed too much of a high-THC chocolate bar (edible). Dowd was not aware that the effects are not immediate and can last for up to several hours. Therefore, for a naïve user, inhalation is the preferable route at least until the proper oral dose is found.

Side Effects Due to Smoking

There are some side effects such as cough, increased sputum production, and/or bronchial irritation which may occur from smoking:

---

[97] "The Science Behind Medical Marijuana: An Interview with Donald Abrams." HealthTalk Live. Last Modified February 2008. https://www.everydayhealth.com/healthy-living/webcasts/the-science-behind-medical-marijuana.aspx/.

[98] "Preventing Reefer Madness." *The Week.* Last Modified June 20, 2014. http://www.antarcticajournal.com/preventing-reefer-madness/.

Cough

Coughing is by far the most common side effect associated with the use of smoked cannabis. This effect is not from cannabis itself, but rather to the route and vehicle of administration, such as when using a cannabis cigarette ("joint"). Using other methods of respiratory administration such as a water pipe (bong) or vaporization device reduces the amount of bronchial irritation, sputum production, and the incidence of cough. Use of sublingual tincture, edibles, or liquids negates the potential problem of cough all together.

Sputum Production

Increased sputum production and bronchial irritation occur with smoked cannabis cigarettes. This is according to the research and presentations of Dr. Donald Tashkin, of UCLA's David Geffen School of Medicine.[99]

Bronchospasm

While bronchospasm can occur, more importantly, cannabis is a bronchodilator. Double-blind experiments conducted by Dr. Tashkin at UCLA using smoked cannabis between 0-2% (0 being the placebo) as well as 15 mg synthetic THC administered orally, found increases in specific airway conductance (bronchodilation) with both smoked and oral methods. He concluded that the broncho-constriction, which might have been expected in asthmatics following inhalation of particulate matter, was not present.[100] The study concluded that THC was effective in relieving exercise-induced bronchospasm. The duration of this bronchodilatory action lasted from four to twelve hours after administration.

In 1977, the same UCLA team used aerosolized THC in 5 mg and 20 mg doses. All doses produced similar, significant bronchodilation. The lower dose produced

---

[99] Tashkin, Donald P. "Effects of marijuana smoking on the lung." *Annals of the American Thoracic Society* 10, no. 3 (2013): 239-247.

[100] Gong, Henry, Donald P. Tashkin, Michael S. Simmons, Barry Calvarese, and Bertrand J. Shapiro. "Acute and subacute bronchial effects of oral cannabinoids." *Clinical Pharmacology & Therapeutics* 35, no. 1 (1984): 26-32.

fewer physical (tachycardia) or psychological (high) side effects than the higher dose or smoked cannabis.[101]

Does Cannabis Cause Lung Cancer?

Smoking cannabis has been associated with assorted respiratory symptoms, increased risk of bronchitis, increased cough, sputum production and bronchial irritation. The suspicion was that cannabis smoking might increase cancer risk, which was only heightened because smoked cannabis does contain carcinogens and is a bronchial irritant. But does cannabis cause lung cancer? Short answer, no, it does not increase the risk of getting lung cancer.

> *Studies indicate that, due to the antiproliferative effect of cannabinoids, cannabis smokers are at a lower risk of developing lung cancer than non-smokers.*

As evidence has mounted about medicinal uses of cannabis, the government has tried to shift their argument for keeping it Schedule I from the argument that cannabis is very bad to the idea that smoking anything is bad. While it sounds reasonable, it turns out that the idea that smoking cannabis causes lung cancer ignores the epidemiology and the science. The DEA's gratuitous statement on April 20, 2006 opposing medical cannabis was couched in repeated references to "smoked marijuana."[102] The DEA has focused more on smoking as a route of administration than the therapeutic potential and therapeutic uses of cannabis, cannabinoids and terpenes.

Cannabis smoke, unlike tobacco, has never been shown to cause lung cancer. In fact, because of the antiproliferative effect of cannabinoids and terpenes, studies indicate that among cannabis users there is a lower risk of cancer than non-

---

[101] Tashkin, Donald P., Sheldon Reiss, Bertrand J. Shapiro, Barry Calvarese, James L. Olsen, and Jon W. Lodge. "Bronchial effects of aerosolized ?9-tetrahydrocannabinol in healthy and asthmatic subjects." *American Review of Respiratory Disease*115, no. 1 (1977): 57-65.
[102] US Food and Drug Administration. "Inter-Agency Advisory Regarding Claims That Smoked Marijuana Is a Medicine, 2014." (2009).

smokers. There are several mechanisms that contribute to cannabis's anti-proliferative effect including inhibiting Angiogenic Growth Factor (AGF), which is emitted by cancer cells while trying to develop their own blood vessels. Additionally, cannabis causes apoptosis in cancer cells.

This lung cancer issue was definitively answered by the 2004 NIDA-funded 2,100-subject study by respected UCLA pulmonology researcher Dr. Donald P. Tashkin. He found that cannabis smokers showed statistically lower cancer rates than non-smokers (i.e., people who smoked nothing at all). Even heavy cannabis smoking did not increase the risk for lung cancer. Tashkin concluded that cannabis smoking—"even heavy long-term use"—does not cause cancer of the lung, upper airways, or esophagus.[103]

This conclusion is especially significant because Tashkin had long believed in the likelihood of a causal relationship of cannabis with lung cancer. This was because of the presence of several carcinogens contained in cannabis smoke and the proven bronchial irritation associated with smoking cannabis. Tashkin's results upset NIDA and even though he had previously received numerous NIDA grants, NIDA worked hard to bury and/or misrepresent the results of his study.

Cardiovascular Effects

A 2002 article by R.T. Jones entitled "Cardiovascular System Effects of Marijuana," points out that tolerance to cardiac effects is rapid. The author states, "With repeated exposure, supine blood pressure decreases slightly, orthostatic hypotension disappears, blood volume increases, heart rate slows, and circulatory responses to exercise and Valsalva maneuver are diminished."[104]

---

[103] Kaufman, Marc. "Study finds no cancer-marijuana connection." *The Washington Post* 26 (2006).

[104] Jones, Reese T. "Cardiovascular system effects of marijuana." *The Journal of Clinical Pharmacology* 42, no. S1 (2002).

Positive Cardiovascular Effects

There are positive cardiovascular effects of cannabis. It helps minimize cell death in an ischemic event. Inflammation has been found to play a central role in vascular occlusions from atrioventricular septal defects (AVSD). Animal research has shown cannabinoids can decrease cardiac damage caused by transient decreased blood flow (e.g., cardiac ischemia).

The beneficial cardiac potential for CBD was highlighted in a 2013 review published in the *Journal of Pharmacology.* The review explains that in rodent models, cannabis reduced vascular tension, a condition that causes additional strain on the heart. Cannabis has also been shown to protect the arteries from damage from glucose. The same article stated that cannabis reduces general inflammation in blood vessels. [105]

The active compounds in cannabis engage with the cardiac system to produce protective effects. A rodent study published in the *International Journal of Cardiology* found deficiencies in the ECS possibly contributing to chronic ASHD. Mice that had lower levels of cannabinoid 1 receptors (CB1) suffered more heart abnormalities than mice with healthy CB1 expression. Researchers "found that CB1 deficiency contributed to the extensive chronic cardiac remodeling... revealing a new role of CB1 in [chronic heart failure]."[106]

CB2 receptor activation is anti-atherogenic. Steffens et. al. showed a decrease in progression of atherosclerotic lesions in murine models after oral administration of

---

[105] Stanley, Christopher P., William H. Hind, and Saoirse E. O'sullivan. "Is the cardiovascular system a therapeutic target for cannabidiol?." *British Journal of Clinical Pharmacology* 75, no. 2 (2013): 313-322.
[106] Liao, Yulin, Jianping Bin, Tao Luo, Hui Zhao, Catherine Ledent, Masanori Asakura, Dingli Xu, Seiji Takashima, and Masafumi Kitakaze. "CB1 cannabinoid receptor deficiency promotes cardiac remodeling induced by pressure overload in mice." *International Journal of Cardiology* 167, no. 5 (2013): 1936-1944.

low-dose THC.[107] THC also downregulates Th1 immune response cells, which are the major cells in atherosclerotic lesions. A synthetic CB2 receptor agonist was shown to decrease the size of plaque and macrophage content in atherosclerotic lesions. The CB2 receptor agonist also reduced oxidized-LDL-mediated NF-kb activation and pro-inflammatory cytokine expression.

In a 15-year longitudinal follow-up of 3,617 adults in the Coronary Artery Risk Development in Young Adults (CARDIA) study, there was no association between cannabis use and cardiovascular risk after adjusting for confounding factors.[108]

IQ Not Affected

In a first of its kind study, scientists analyzed long-term cannabis users by comparing identical twins. Researchers compared IQ changes in twin siblings who either used or abstained from cannabis for 10 years. After taking environmental factors into account, in over 3,000 individuals the scientists found **no measurable link between cannabis use and lower IQ.**[109] This is in contrast to the much smaller studies that report a negative correlation between cannabis smoking and IQ levels.[110, 111] The participant size in these studies combined was less than 125 individuals.

---

[107] Steffens, Sabine, Niels R. Veillard, Claire Arnaud, Graziano Pelli, Fabienne Burger, Christian Staub, Andreas Zimmer, Jean-Louis Frossard, and François Mach. "Low dose oral cannabinoid therapy reduces progression of atherosclerosis in mice." *Nature* 434, no. 7034 (2005): 782.

[108] Rodondi, Nicolas, Mark James Pletcher, Kiang Liu, Stephen Benjamin Hulley, and Stephen Sidney. "Marijuana use, diet, body mass index, and cardiovascular risk factors (from the CARDIA study)." *American Journal of Cardiology* 98, no. 4 (2006): 478-484.

[109] Jackson, Nicholas J., Joshua D. Isen, Rubin Khoddam, Daniel Irons, Catherine Tuvblad, William G. Iacono, Matt McGue, Adrian Raine, and Laura A. Baker. "Impact of adolescent marijuana use on intelligence: Results from two longitudinal twin studies." *Proceedings of the National Academy of Sciences* 113, no. 5 (2016): E500-E508.

[110] Lyons, Michael J., J. L. Bar, M. S. Panizzon, R. Toomey, S. Eisen, H. Xian, and M. T. Tsuang. "Neuropsychological consequences of regular marijuana use: a twin study." *Psychological Medicine* 34, no. 7 (2004): 1239-1250.

[111] Fried, Peter, Barbara Watkinson, Deborah James, and Robert Gray. "Current and former marijuana use: preliminary findings of a longitudinal study of effects on IQ in young adults." *Canadian Medical Association Journal* 166, no. 7 (2002): 887-891.

"This is a very well-conducted study...and a welcome addition to the literature," says Valerie Curran, a psycho-pharmacologist at the University College London. She and her colleagues reached "broadly the same conclusions" in a separate, non-twin study of more than 2,000 British teenagers.[112]

Unhigh

Whether smoking a high-THC cannabis strain for the first time, or eating a product more potent than you are used to, or using RSO for cancer getting too stoned (e.g., dysphoria) is something that happens to many people.

Both THC and CBD doseage effects a cannabis consumer's experience. Beginners are most susceptible to dysphoria, but while this can be uncomfortable it is not a life-threatening or permanent problem. Here are some common approaches.

What Can You Do?

There are several things you can do that may mitigate or avoid this unpleasant high. These include:

- **Dosing**
  Start with a low dose of whole plant THC extract, maybe 2.5 mg. Slowly increase the dose in half grain increments.

- **CBD**
  Unless treating pain, where more   than 1:1 THC:CBD can interfere with analgesia, increase the CBD dose. CBD particularly blocks the euphoria associated with cannabis.

- **Other useful drugs besides CBD**
  Terepenes
  Ibuprofen
  Citicoline

---

112 Underwood, Emily. "Twins Study Finds No Evidence that Marijuana Lowers IQ in Teens." *Science Magazine*. January 18, 2016.
http://www.sciencemag.org/news/2016/01/twins-study-finds-no-evidence-marijuana-lowers-iq-teens

- **Other non-pharmacological actions**
  Use suppository route of administration
  Bathe or shower
  Hydrate

CHAPTER 14
PREGNANCY

Cannabis in Pregnancy

The effect of maternal cannabis use in pregnancy on the developing fetus is controversial. The American College of Obstetricians and Gynecologists recommends that pregnant or breast-feeding women—and women considering pregnancy— should be screened for and discouraged from using cannabis and other substances. There is not one gold standard study demonstrating significant adverse effects. There are other studies which show no effect on the fetus and some that show a benefit.

Ciara A. Torres of Columbia University reviewed over thirty studies on prenatal use of cannabis. Most were funded by NIDA. There were over 380 variables. Only eight of the variables in all of these studies were abnormal or negative, but there was no consistency in these negative findings. Furthermore, many of the results were positive, but you couldn't tell what the findings really were because the write-ups, according to Dr. Torres, were slanted to reporting what researchers seemed to think the funding source wanted to hear. [113]

Because of the problems caused by confounding findings and routine lack of control of these factors (nutrition, environments, other drug use), we cannot say with certainty that cannabis has any adverse effects on the developing fetus and while we can't say it doesn't, we can say that there is no unequivocal compelling scientific evidence or epidemiologic evidence that demonstrates it. As with the ingestion of any

---

[113] ACOG Committee Opinion". The American College of Obstetricians and Gynaecologists. Last Modified October 2017. https://www.acog.org/Clinical-Guidance-and-Publications/Committee-Opinions/Committee-on-Obstetric-Practice/Marijuana-Use-During-Pregnancy-and-Lactation

therapeutic agent during pregnancy, cannabis should be used with caution.

NIDA Study in Jamaica

The idea that THC is deleterious to the developing mind has never been shown to be a fact. Melody Dreher, RN, PhD, did a series of NIDA-funded studies in Jamaica in 1968 and in 1973. Dreher compared children of women who had used cannabis during pregnancy against children of women who had not. Dr. Dreher's study demonstrated no problems for children whose mothers used cannabis during pregnancy and in fact showed that these children of cannabis-using mothers performed better in school and met developmental landmarks sooner than children of non-cannabis-using mothers. Her study in Jamaica, therefore, found that there were no adverse effects to the child if a mother had used cannabis in pregnancy and or while breast feeding.[114]

She used the Brazelton Neonatal Behavioral Assessment Scale to compare the babies of 24 Jamaican women who had used ganja. At one month, the children of the cannabis users had better scores than the non-cannabis users, which the researchers attributed to "the cultural positioning and social and economic characteristics of mothers using marijuana that select for the use of cannabis but also promote neonatal development."

She did ethnographic studies which examined the lifestyles of mothers who used ganja and mothers who didn't use ganja (Indian name for combination of flowering tops and leaves) and compared behavioral characteristics of neonates from both groups in the first month of life. She and her research team went back five years later and did a five-year follow-up study on the children.

Her studies are among the few which actually measured how much ganja (cannabis) a woman consumed. Dr. Dreher

---

[114] Torres, Ciara A., and Carl L. Hart. "Prenatal cannabis exposure and cognitive functioning: A critical review." *Drug & Alcohol Dependence* 171 (2017): e204.

noted that she "wasn't sitting in a clinic somewhere divorced from women's lives asking them how much marijuana they'd used."[115] Her research team was in a community and in the field where they observed these women and checked out their reports. Her team knew how much ganja, and what type and potency, they were consuming.

When NIDA saw the results were favorable to cannabis they ceased funding the study. The overwhelming consensus in the cannabinoid medicine community, however, is that the research findings of Dr. Melanie Dreher were profound and far-reaching.

Other Studies and Their Findings

- No difference in birth weight, shorter birth length, smaller head circumference [116] (BJOG 2002; 109:21-7)
- Writing in their 1997 book (The Lindesmith Center), Drs. John P. Morgan and Lynn Zimmer assert "Marijuana has no reliable impact on birth size, length of gestation...or the occurrence of physical abnormalities."[117]
- A 1999 study in Copenhagen concluded that "the use of cannabis is not a major prognostic factor regarding the outcome of pregnancy."[118]
- A 2002 survey of 12,060 British women did not demonstrate significant differences in growth among newborns exposed to cannabis in utero versus those with no exposure, when controlling for co-founding factors such as the mother's age, pre-pregnancy weight, and the self-reported use of tobacco, alcohol,

[115] Dreher, Melanie C., Kevin Nugent, and Rebekah Hudgins. "Prenatal marijuana exposure and neonatal outcomes in Jamaica: an ethnographic study." *Pediatrics* 93, no. 2 (1994): 254-260.

[116] Fergusson, David M., L. John Horwood, and Kate Northstone. "Maternal use of cannabis and pregnancy outcome." *BJOG: An International Journal of Obstetrics & Gynaecology* 109, no. 1 (2002): 21-27.

[117] Morgan, John P., and Lynn Zimmer. "Exposing marijuana myths: A review of the scientific evidence." *Cannabis Science/Cannabis Wissenschaft*. Frankfurt Am Main: Peter Lang Verlag (1997): 101-126.

[118] Balle, J., M. J. Olofsson, and J. Hilden. "Cannabis and pregnancy." *Ugeskr Laeger* 161, no. 36 (1999): 5024-8.

caffeine, cocaine after controlling for maternal tobacco usage.[119]

- A 1997 Australian study of 32,483 mothers also reported, "There is inadequate evidence that cannabis, at the amount typically consumed by pregnant women, causes low birth weight."[120] Most recently, a large-scale case-control study published in the journal Pediatric and Perinatal Epidemiology determined that mothers who reported using cannabis during pregnancy suffered no increased risk of bearing children with acute myeloid leukemia, a cancer known to occur in adolescents under age 15.[121]

Summary of Prenatal Cannabis Exposure on Short-Term Effects: Birth Outcome Are Mixed and Inconclusive

PURPORTED EFFECT	EVIDENCE
Preterm delivery	Mixed evidence
Low birth weight/SGA	Mixed evidence
Fetal growth	Mixed evidence
Withdrawal	No effect

Limitations of Studies

Because of limitations, the studies that have been done to address this issue are not gold standard double blind studies. The fact is that it's much easier to do studies on mice than it is on humans. This is because there are many confounding factors. These confounding factors include, but are not limited to:

- Environmental risk factors
- Family history

---

[119] Fergusson, David M., L. John Horwood, and Kate Northstone. "Maternal use of cannabis and pregnancy outcome." *BJOG: An International Journal of Obstetrics & Gynaecology* 109, no. 1 (2002): 21-27.

[120] English, D. R., G. K. Hulse, E. Milne, C. D. J. Holman, and C. I. Bower. "Maternal cannabis use and birth weight: a meta-analysis." *Addiction* 92, no. 11 (1997): 1553-1560.

[121] Trivers, Katrina F., Ann C. Mertens, Julie A. Ross, Michael Steinbuch, Andrew F. Olshan, and Leslie L. Robison. "Parental marijuana use and risk of childhood acute myeloid leukaemia: a report from the Children's Cancer Group (United States and Canada)." *Paediatric and Perinatal Epidemiology* 20, no. 2 (2006): 110-118.

- Maternal IQ/cognitive ability
- Socioeconomic status
- Recruitment methods
- Assessment measures
- Medical Issues (PTSD, ADD, TBI)
- Drug Use (alcohol, tobacco, cocaine, heroin, Rx)

Conclusion Regarding Pre-Natal Exposure to Cannabinoids

Cannabis does not have any well-documented adverse impact on a developing fetus. Dreher's work from Jamaica examined the birth weights and early development of babies exposed to cannabis compared to non-exposed infants. (Mothers in the study reported that they occasionally mixed cannabis with tea as an alternative to smoking.) Her study reported no significant physical or psychological differences in newborns of heavy cannabis-using mothers at three days old and found that exposed children performed better on a variety of physiological and autonomic tests than non-exposed children at 30 days. (This latter trend was suggested to have been a result of the socio-economic status of the mothers rather than a result of pre-natal cannabis exposure.)

CHAPTER 15
CANNABIS DEPENDENCE

Though scientific evidence has proven cannabis dependency to be real, this dependency has been overhyped, overplayed, and exaggerated. Dependency risk associated with cannabis is, in fact, less than that of coffee. In 1953, Thompson and Proctor summed up the attitude of the great majority of the medical profession stating, "the use of cannabis does not give rise to biological or physiological dependence and discontinuance of the drug does not result in withdrawal symptoms."[122]

In 1976, Stephen Szara of NIDA categorically stated, "the question of physical dependence...has been answered with a flat no. No physical dependence, of the type seen in opiates, has been seen in man and this is true even today."[123] It is easier to stop using cannabis than it is to stop drinking coffee or smoking nicotine containing substances.

The Institute of Medicine concluded in their report in 1999, "Experimental animals that are given the opportunity to self-administer cannabinoids generally do not choose to do so, which has led to the conclusion that they (e.g., cannabinoids) are not reinforcing or rewarding. The IOM report states there is a very low incidence of cannabis "dependence." They reasoned, "Millions of Americans have tried marijuana, but most are not regular user ...[and] few marijuana users become dependent on it."[124]

It should come as little surprise then that most cannabis users without a diagnosis of a chronic or fatal illness voluntarily cease their cannabis smoking by their late 20s or

---

[122] Grivas, Kleanthis, and Deborah Whitehouse. *Cannabis: Marihuana-Hashish*. Minerva Press, 1997.

[123] Ibid.

[124] Joy, Janet, Stanley J. Watson, Jr., and John A. Benson, eds. *Marijuana and Medicine: Assessing the Science Base*. Washington D.C.: National Academy Press, 1999.

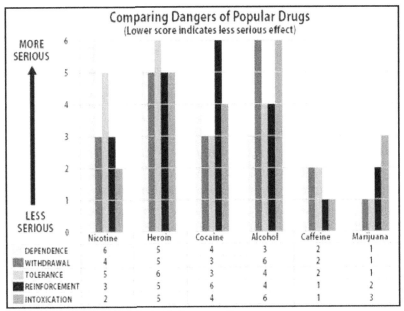

Comparing Dangers of Popular Drugs
(Lower score indicates less serious effect)

	Nicotine	Heroin	Cocaine	Alcohol	Caffeine	Marijuana
DEPENDENCE	6	5	4	3	2	1
WITHDRAWAL	4	5	3	6	2	1
TOLERANCE	5	6	3	4	2	1
REINFORCEMENT	3	5	6	4	1	2
INTOXICATION	2	5	4	6	1	3

http://drugwarfacts.org/chapter/addictive_properties

early 30s, often citing health or professional concerns and/or the decision to start a family. Contrast this pattern with that of the typical tobacco smoker, many of whom start as teens and continue smoking daily for the rest of their lives.

Experts Have Determined Cannabis Dependency Risk Is Less Than Coffee

When dependency risk for cannabis is compared to other substances including coffee, cannabis is considered by experts to have the lowest dependency risk and therefore be the safest. A 1994 New York Times article cites work by Drs. Jack Henningfield, then with NIDA, and Neal Benowitz of the University of California at San Francisco. Henningfield and Benowitz rated the addictive symptoms of cannabis vs. other commonly used drugs including heroin, alcohol, nicotine, coffee and cocaine.

Overall, "Marijuana was ranked lowest for withdrawal symptoms, tolerance and dependence (addiction) potential; it ranked close to caffeine in the degree of reinforcement and higher than caffeine and nicotine only in the degree of intoxication." It has also been reported that, "Even in cases of high daily intake, such as the 94-day study of high dose cannabis, with its sudden cessation; withdrawal symptoms were transient and mild."[125]

In fact, authors of the report found less than 10% of marijuana users ever exhibited symptoms of dependence as defined by the American Psychiatric Association's DSM 3 criteria. By comparison, 15% of alcohol users, 17% of cocaine users and a whopping 32% of cigarette smokers statistically exhibited symptoms of drug dependence.[126]

Mild Withdrawal Symptoms

A study by Reese Jones, M.D., a critic of medical cannabis, was designed in the hopes of demonstrating withdrawal symptoms from THC. He placed volunteers on 210 mg of dronabinol (synthetic THC) a day for 20 days. This medicine, containing only THC, has none of the hundreds of other naturally occurring plant compounds that would help balance the effects of THC-induced euphoria. This study's daily dose is equivalent to smoking 20-40 joints of natural cannabis per day. At the end of 30 days, the THC was stopped abruptly. This is a formula calculated to maximize any drug's withdrawal symptoms. He was disappointed to find only mild withdrawal symptoms in individuals taking the large doses of synthetic $\triangle$-9-THC under laboratory conditions.

The 210 mg/day that Dr. Jones subjects were given is far higher (15-30x) than what would be consumed by the average medicinal cannabis consumer. Benowitz and Jones reported initial tachycardia and hypertension in volunteer subjects. These effects were short-lived as they found tolerance develops to tachycardia and the central nervous system effects over the

[125] Lambert, Didier M., ed. *Cannabinoids in Nature and Medicine.* John Wiley & Sons, 2009.
[126] Ibid.

20-day experiment. In general, participants' blood pressure reduced and stabilized at around 95/65 mm Hg.[127]

Cannabis Dependency

There certainly is the condition of drug dependency. It can be a symptom of some underlying condition such as anxiety, PTSD, Endocannabinoid Deficiency Syndrome and/or depression. If present these motivating conditions must be addressed. Substance dependency is defined as using ia substance in such a manner that the consumption of that substance interferes with important aspects of a person's life be it financial, occupational, educational, recreational, social, familial or other important parts of living life.

Treating drug dependency as an isolated condition without treating the underlying cause is a recipe for treatment failure. On the other hand, addressing the motivation for excessive and or inappropriate substance use can be helpful in promoting a successful outcome.

There is a dependency risk to most recreational drugs and many of pharmaceutical agents. Of the recreational drugs cannabis has the least dependency risk. Drug dependency is determined by several factors including (1) how difficult it is for the user to quit using the drug, (2) the relapse rate, (3) the percentage of people who eventually become dependent.

The term dependency is a rather vague term that can be arbitrarily applied. Cannabis is an example of that arbitrariness.

Dependency is a problem common to prescription medication like tranquilizers and pain medication. Cannabis has a dependency risk, but experts have said it is less than coffee and therefore is much lower than prescription pain medicine or any anxiolytic. The fact that dependency may occur is not a reason

---

[127] Jones, Reese T., Neal L. Benowitz and Ronald I. Herning. "Clinical relevance of cannabis tolerance and dependence." *The Journal of Clinical Pharmacology* 21, no. S1 (1981).

not to use a drug having medicinal benefits and few side effects under the supervision of a physician.

As mentioned earlier, doctors are trained to balance side effects versus therapeutic effects in determining whether to prescribe or recommend a particular treatment. Cannabis' low side-effect profile is what makes it such an attractive therapeutic agent to physicians knowledgeable in the science of cannabinoid medicine. Doctors also are trained and experienced in monitoring appropriate drug use.

Cannabis Use Disorder

Psychiatric diagnoses are categorized by the American Psychiatric Association in their *Diagnostic and Statistical Manual of Mental Disorders* (DSM). The manual, better known as the DSM 5, covers all mental health disorders for both children and adults. In the newest edition, the 5th, the APA has redefined their section on cannabis. The DSM 5 lists something called "cannabis use disorder." The definition is only somewhat different than for "cannabis abuse" that appeared in the previous edition of this manual, the DSM 4(IV).

In assessing the cannabis related definitions such as use disorder it is important to recognize that the symptoms are almost entirely related to the recreational use of the drug and not the therapeutic use. Also some of these diagnoses and symptoms are influenced by the fact that per the 1970 Controlled Substances Act, the legal status of cannabis is as a Schedule I drug.

The DSM 5 defines use disorder as, "A problematic pattern of cannabis use leading to clinically significant impairment or distress, as manifested by at least 2 of the following, occurring within a 12-month period:"[128]

- Cannabis is often taken in larger amounts or over a longer period than was intended.
- There is a persistent desire or unsuccessful efforts to cut down or control cannabis use.

---

[128] *Diagnostic and Statistic Manual of Mental Disorders*, 5th Edition. American Psychiatric Association, 2013.

- A great deal of time is spent in activities necessary to obtain cannabis, use cannabis, or recover from its effects.

  The first two items here are largely related to cannabis' legal status. With the changing legal climate the criteria is occurring less often.

- Craving, or a strong desire or urge to use cannabis.
- Recurrent cannabis use resulting in a failure to fulfill major role obligations at work, school, or home.
- Continued cannabis use despite having persistent or recurrent social or interpersonal problems caused or exacerbated by the effects of cannabis.
- Important social, occupational, or recreational activities are given up or reduced because of cannabis use.
- Recurrent cannabis use in situations in which it is physically hazardous. Cannabis use is continued despite knowledge of having a persistent or recurrent physical or psychological problem that is likely to have been caused or exacerbated by cannabis.
- Tolerance, as defined by either a (1) need for markedly increased cannabis to achieve intoxication or desired effect or (2) markedly diminished effect with continued use of the same amount of the substance.

  Tolerance is a rarity with cannabis: it is fat soluble, so a regular consumer of cannabis has some THC stored in their adipose tissue; there are no or only mild withdrawal symptoms, and, while tolerance to side effects may occur, most recreational users do not increase their dose to achieve a high.

- Withdrawal, per the DSMS 5 withdrawal, is
  - the characteristic withdrawal syndrome for cannabis or,

o   cannabis is taken to relieve or avoid withdrawal symptoms.[129]

Cannabis Use Disorder Considerations

Whatever we call it or however we define it, the symptoms associated with cannabis use disorder deserve to be addressed. Like any medical issue it should be treated by health personnel, not the police. Both patients and physicians should be alert for the unhelpful use of cannabis. This use may have started out as recreational or as an adolescent act of defiance or independence. It may also be associated with an effort to deal with the symptoms of ADD or PTSD. These issues often arise in early adolescence and must be considered in diagnosing cannabis use disorder.

That said, cannabis dependency is often easy to treat. While it has been stated that 5-10% of cannabis users may have dependency, those numbers may be over-estimated. They ignore that many regular cannabis users are consuming cannabis for medicinal purposes and therefore do not meet the criteria for dependence.

In order to focus treatment resources on those with substance abuse issues it is important to distinguish use from abuse. Few would argue with assisting and treating someone whose life is problematic and drug abuse has been a contributing factor. Such abuse occurs but is rarely seen in the medical use of cannabis. The vast majority of people who are prescribed or recommended therapeutic use of psychoactive drugs take them appropriately with the same or fewer side effects than many other categories of drug. This is certainly true of the low side-effect profile of cannabis.[130]

While there no doubt there is something that can identified as cannabis dependence (relying too heavily on cannabis to deal with problems of the day), there is no such thing as a classical addiction to cannabis.

---

[129] *Diagnostic and Statistic Manual of Mental Disorders*, 5th Edition. American Psychiatric Association, 2013.
[130] "Your Government is Lying to You (Again) About Marijuana." NORML. http://norml.org/library/item/your-government-is-lying-to-you-again-about-marijuana

CHAPTER 16
DRIVING

No Relationship Between Blood THC Levels and Psychomotor Impairment

The National Highway Traffic Safety Administration's (NHTSA) online factsheet states, "It is difficult to establish a relationship between a person's THC blood or plasma concentration and performance impairing effects....It is inadvisable to try and predict effects based on blood THC concentrations alone, and currently impossible to predict specific effects based on THC [carbolic acid] COOH concentrations." The NHTSA found no increased risk of auto accident from use of cannabis, and stated that cannabis may lead to slower, more careful driving.

The Food and Drug Administration (FDA) Warning

The FDA is unconcerned about THC levels and driving. Their concern is whether THC in the blood impairs driving. The FDA does not believe that the mere presence of the cannabinoid THC or its metabolites in a patient's blood stream is an absolute contraindication to driving, operating heavy equipment or engaging in dangerous activity. The FDA warning is a clear and very significant statement:

> "WARNING: Patients receiving treatment with MARINOL® Capsules should be specifically warned not to drive, operate machinery, or engage in any hazardous activity until it is established that they are able to tolerate the drug and to perform such tasks safely."[131]

---

[131] "Cannabis/Marijuana (△-9-Tetrahydrocannabinol, THC)." National Highway Traffic Safety Administration.
https://www.nhtsa.gov/sites/nhtsa.dot.gov/files/documents/812440-marijuana-impaired-driving-report-to-congress.pdf

The FDA-approved warning clearly states that it is permissible to drive, operate heavy equipment, or engage in dangerous activities so long as the use of THC (dronabinol) does not interfere with those activities. So, according to the FDA, it is permissible to drive a motor vehicle without reference to blood THC levels.

Many physicians put some form of this FDA driving warning on their recommendation. You might add the phrase. "Don't drive if you are and/or feel impaired." If a medicinal cannabis patient gets in a serious accident and they can be proven to be impaired, the legal risks and consequences can be devastating. Make sure the patient is aware that they should take the FDA admonition to heart.

When talking to your patients regarding cannabis and driving, the safest and best advice here is to follow the standard warning.

While many of my patients do not feel medicinal use of cannabis impairs their driving, others feel it may or does and refrain from medicating only when they are finished driving for the day. Even if a patient is not impaired, many jurisdictions are quick to charge the patient if the odor of cannabis is in the car, on the patient's clothing, or if there is cannabis or paraphernalia somewhere. A driver must use the same common sense as they would with prescription drugs and alcohol.

Some people find it difficult to process this FDA conclusion. Part of the difficulty in absorbing it is that this requires recognizing the fact that alcohol differs from most other psychoactive substances. It does not bind to specific receptors. It is a non-specific neural depressant.

In 2014, the NHTSA stated, "The alcohol laws are based on evidence concerning the decreased ability of drivers across the population to function safely at these [blood alcohol content levels]....Such evidence is not currently available for concentrations of other drugs."[132] Most medications, including cannabinoids, act by affecting specific receptors. Also, there is considerable human variability, so some people have more side effects than others. And in some people, the cannabinoids are more effective than in others.

Department of Transportation / National Highway Traffic Safety Administration

The U.S. Department of Transportation (DOT) has said, "It is not possible to conclude anything about a driver's impairment on the basis of his/her plasma concentrations of THC and THC-COOH determined in a single sample."[133]

Tolerance is a contributor to an important conclusion in the February 2015 and 1993 NHTSA reports. The NHTSA findings underscore an important point: "the measurable presence of THC (cannabis's primary active ingredient) in a person's system doesn't correlate with impairment in the same way that alcohol concentration does."

The 2015 NHTSA report doesn't mince words: "At the current time, specific drug concentration levels cannot be reliably equated with a specific degree of driver impairment."[134] Little appears to have changed from the National Highway Traffic Administration 1993 Safety Study Report, which stated, "THC's adverse effects on driving performance appear relatively small" and "Evidence from the present and previous studies strongly suggests that alcohol encourages risky driving, whereas THC encourages greater caution."[135]

---

132 National Highway Traffic Safety Administration. Op. cit.

133 "Marijuana and Actual Driving Performance, Effects of THC on Driving Performance," U.S. Department of Transportation, NHTSA, November 1993.
http://druglibrary.org/schaffer/misc/driving/dot78_1.htm/.

134 Ingraham, Christopher. "Stone Drivers are a lot safer than drunk ones, new federal data show." *The Washington Post*. February 9, 2015.
https://www.washingtonpost.com/news/wonk/wp/2015/02/09/stoned-drivers-are-a-lot-safer-than-drunk-ones-new-federal-data-show/?utm_term=.f7f307bb0840/.

135 Robbe, H. W. J. "Marijuana's effects on actual driving performance." Adelaide, Australia: Kloeden C, McLean AJ, editors (1995).

An article by C.T. Lamers states, "Performance as rated on the Driving Proficiency Scale did not differ between treatments (cannabis versus placebo). It was concluded that the effects of low doses of THC...on visual search and general driving proficiency are minimal." Using driving instructors' performance scores, Lamers and Ramaekers found essentially no differences between the dosed and non-dosed conditions.[136]

Residual Levels of THC

This is something clinicians who recommend cannabis medicine need to be aware of since one or more of their patients may be charged with driving under the influence (DUI) of cannabis. This may occur even though the police report provides documentation to the contrary. This false charge can be related to elevated blood THC levels resulting from the fat solubility of cannabinoids and the fact that many law enforcement officers are ill-informed regarding cannabis, cannabinoids and the endocannabinoid system.

There are many studies out there that document the phenomenon of THC accumulating in the adipose tissue and then being released slowly back into the bloodstream. Agurell et al. studied THC levels in one "heavy marijuana user". His plasma THC was measured each day for four days before and one hour after smoking one cigarette laced with 10 mg radioactively labeled THC, and for eight days after ceasing all use. Prior to the experiment his plasma THC was roughly 20mg/ml. The levels of labeled and unlabeled THC both rose after smoking each cigarette, indicating the existing THC may be displaced from the fatty tissues as fresh THC is absorbed.[137]

---

[136] Lamers, Caroline TJ, and Johannes Gerardus Ramaekers. "Visual search and urban driving under the influence of marijuana and alcohol." *Human Psychopharmacology: Clinical and Experimental* 16, no. 5 (2001): 393-401.

[137] Lindgren, Jan-Erik, Agneta Ohlsson, Stig Agurell, Leo Hollister, and Hamp Gillespie. "Clinical effects and plasma levels of $\triangle$- 9-tetrahydrocannabinol ($\triangle$-9-THC) in heavy and light users of cannabis." *Psychopharmacology* 74, no. 3 (1981): 208-212.

CHAPTER 17
TOXICOLOGY

Hair Sample Toxicology

Hair samples show a six-month history of substance use. A toxicology result shows the presence or absence of a drug or its principle metabolite. It is NOT by itself evidence of substance abuse. It does not distinguish use from abuse nor does it indicate the nature and reason for that substance use. A positive test for opiates in a patient prescribed opiates does NOT in any way justify a diagnosis of drug abuse.

Urine Testing

Applicable federal and state law is clear that it is okay if you get your cannabinoid from prescription dronabinol (synthetic △-9-THC), but not okay if you get your cannabinoids from the cannabis plant, which contains over 100 different cannabinoids, plus terpenes, flavonoids and phenoids. So, the California Supreme Court says if THC is discovered in a worker's urine and it came from the plant, not the pill, they can be fired; that is because THC is a prescription medicine and cannabis is not.[138]

You might ask, what does dronabinol have to do with testing positive for marijuana? The answer is that the blood and urine tests used by commercial laboratories to detect marijuana are not a test for marijuana but a test for THC and two of its principle metabolites, 9-carboxy-THC and 11-hydroxy-THC. The reasoning here is that the toxicology screen is looking for the presence of illicit drugs not licit drugs. Thus, per the Medical Review Officers Association guidelines, it is okay if a urine or blood toxicology test was positive for THC and/or its

---

[138] *Ross v. Ragingwire Telecommunications, Inc.*, 70 Cal. Rptr. 3d 382 (2008). https://www.kmm.com/articles-391.html

metabolites because of taking dronabinol, but it is not okay if the same test results come from using marijuana. The very same substance—THC—can either result in termination or not, depending on whether the THC came from a prescription or a recommendation. A second test for THCV must be done to rule out cannabis as the source of THC. This is an additional expense and is rarely done.

Remember that the presence of THC and its metabolites doesn't indicate impairment. It indicates that cannabis was consumed sometime in the last four to seven days. So, if someone becomes nauseated and takes cannabis on a Saturday, they can be fired come Monday if they are drug-tested. Something seems wrong here.

Medical Review Officers (MRO) Association Guidelines for Interpreting Presence of THC

In a little-noted but potentially significant fact, the toxicology interpretation guides for medical review officers (MROs), the physicians responsible for interpreting the results of employee urinalysis, are instructed to report those testing positive for THC as negative if the subject is being legally prescribed THC (dronabinol). This guideline treats synthetic THC the same as one would any other prescribed medication. For instance, a positive for opiates/hydrocodone in a patient prescribed Norco, which contains hydrocodone, would be reported as a negative.[140++]

---

[139] "Medical Review Officers." U.S. Department of Transportation.
https://www.transportation.gov/odapc/mro/.

CHAPTER 18
CLINICAL STANDARDS

How extensive should a physician visit be when recommending other nonprescription, alternative or complementary therapies or OTCs or medical appliances such as turmeric, kratom, a knee brace, aspirin, Feldenkrais, acupuncture and the like? Unfortunately, the answer is up to the whim of regional medical boards, whether the board views a doctor as a primary care physician or a cannabinoid medicine specialist and whether the DEA is breathing down the board's neck.

As the executive vice-president of the American Academy of Cannabinoid Medicine (AACM) and former medical director and director of the Health Services Department of the Santa Barbara Regional Health Authority (SBRHA, now known as "CenCal Health"), it is my opinion that in many cases the recommending physician is not acting as a primary care physician but as a specialist in much the same way as a physician operating within a methadone maintenance clinic setting.

The problem is that it is very subjective as to what standards are appropriate for an alternative or complementary medical treatment and what the Board requires. Since this is wide open to interpretation, physicians recommending cannabis need to practice and document a little on the conservative side. From my 14 years as medical director of SBRHA/CenCal, I am aware of the wide variability of medical practice standards and the subjective application and nature of such standards.

There are several practice standards out there. It appears that some U.S. states and local regions apply these standards with great vigor when recommending cannabis for medicinal use.

Patient Evaluation

A documented in-person medical evaluation and collection of relevant clinical history should include patient's history of present illness, past medical and surgical history, alcohol and other substance use history, physical exam, plus the diagnosis that requires the marijuana recommendation.

- **Physician-Patient Relationship**

  The *Association of Medical Boards* says the following regarding guidelines:

  > Physicians must have documented that an appropriate physician-patient relationship has been established, prior to providing a recommendation, attestation, or authorization for marijuana to the patient.

  The *Medical Board of California (MBC)* Guidelines for Recommending Cannabis
  - o Bonafide doctor-patient relationship
  - o Good faith History and Physical
  - o Review records
  - o Plan with objectives
  - o A condition which will benefit from use of cannabis

Having been the medical director of the oldest county-organized, Medicaid-managed care program in the country for 14 years, I take issue with having a plan with objectives. That is not information required by the California State Health Department for Medicaid-managed care programs.

- **Vital Signs**

  The medical exam is more complete with vital signs. That said, my urologist has never taken my pulse or blood pressure or temperature. That does not make him a bad urologist. My advice is to do pulse, weight and blood pressure.

My Practice Pattern

Doctors all have different standards that they hold themselves to. At times with cannabis medicine I find myself practicing defensive medicine for medico-legal reasons. Currently, that includes pre-visit screening, getting the patient's relevant old medical records, written and oral history, providing the patient a brief overview on medicinal cannabis, including discussion of side effects and routes of administration. I also cover dosage and define what are THC, CBD other cannabinoids, terpenes, and dronabinol. I also discuss the option to not utilize cannabis-based medicine and possible other alternative treatments. This is a very prudent way to make recommendations in a new patient.

The best advice in practicing cannabinoid medicine is to treat cannabis and cannabinoids as any other therapeutic agent. Remember, cannabis has been a known medicine for at least 4,000 years and as late as the 1930's was in millions of prescriptions written by American physicians. The following is an outline of the important suggested elements:

I. Pre-Visit Screening:

I suggest pre-visit screening of all new applicants, and request that they bring all their supporting documents to verify their diagnosis and/or symptomatology that brings them to inquire about cannabis as a treatment.

We screen all potential new cannabinoid medicine patients on the phone. We ask them for their diagnosis and what documentation they have, the treatment they have received and the last time they sought medical attention for the condition they are seeking the cannabis recommendation for.

II. Have Educational Material in The Waiting Room:
A. Handouts
B. Videos
  1. "Medicinal Cannabis and Its Impact on Your Health"
  2. "Cannabis and Cannabinoids in the 21st Century"
C. Have educational materials assembled to give the patient on mechanism of action, the endo-cannabinoid system, cannabis, cannabinoids and terpenes.

III. Appointment Length:
First appointment should take between 25 to 60 minutes, depending upon complexity of the case. By having "Medicinal Cannabis Use and Its Impact on Your Health" available in the waiting room, this might cut a few minutes off the visit.

IV. History:
We require patients to bring both old records and complete a multi-page history form. I also take an oral history from the patient at the time of the visit.

V. Physical Exam:
Perform a reasonable general physical, including vital signs, with particular examination of the body part or organ system principally involved in the patient's state/medical condition.

VI. Follow-up and referral as medically appropriate:
A. Make appropriate referrals when indicated.
B. Send consultation reports, progress notes and care plans to specialists who are actively involved in the patients' management as a matter of continuity of care.

VII. Practice Good Medicine:
Doctors who practice good medicine have little to worry about when choosing to recommend cannabis. Chances are, patients will not have a problem with law

enforcement, but we are still in the waning days of "Reefer Madness" so on some occasions, doctors may need to testify in support of their patients in court. Don't dwell on that as a possible big drain on your professional time. The necessity for going to court to explain medicinal cannabis is becoming rarer and the time is billable. It is also par for the course as a doctor choosing to utilize cannabis in their patient's treatment.

VIII. Record Keeping:

Keep good records. This is your best protection against an over-zealous medical board. Do adequate documentation. I got into the field of cannabinoid medicine because of doing expert witness work. Both my history-taking and chart documentation is done with the possibility that I might need to rely on these records in court. There is often a distinction between chart notes required or expected of a specialist and those of a primary care provider. The consultant often zeros in mainly on the specific specialist issues before them. In this context we are looking primarily at whether the patient has a condition that could possibly benefit from the use of cannabis. There needs to be sufficient documentation to justify making such a recommendation.

Educational Discussion

There are many misconceptions about cannabis. Remember, patients and physicians alike have grown up having been presented with misinformation and falsehoods regarding cannabis, cannabinoids and the endocannabinoid system. It can help the patient feel at ease by framing medicinal cannabis by history, modern clinical use and science. Those who have experience using cannabis recreationally may think they understand the medical applications. While some long-time recreational users may have a solid foundation for understanding medical use, many do not.

At least until 2017 many patients, particularly older patients, have been put off by the stigma that was attached to cannabis by William Randolph Hearst, the petrochemical industry, and Richard Nixon. Discussion with and education of the patient helps relieve many unsubstantiated fears. I give my patients an overview of the applicable law and the science and attempt to answer all their questions.

Following are topics I typically cover in their discussion:
- The voluntary medical cannabis identification state card
- The science of ECS and cannabis
- The dose and route of administration
- The common side effects
- Retrograde inhibition effect of endocannabinoids
- Explain the mechanism of action of retrograde inhibition

Data Needed to Document Justification for Recommendation

How much data a physician needs to know to and/or begin to surmise and eventually conclude that a patient would benefit from the use of cannabis for medical purposes varies, but the information required is relatively straight forward. This information includes:
- The patient diagnosis and/or medical condition
- A medical history
- Medical records supporting that diagnosis
- Possible physical exam supporting this diagnosis.
  Note that for many diagnosis (e.g. anxiety, sleep issues, obsessive compulsive disorder, migraines, seizure disorder, etc) there may not be any physical findings. In such instances past medical treatment and history are more significant.
- It may be helpful to determine what previous treatment (e.g. surgery, physical therapy, prescription

medication, counseling) the patient has previously received.

- If the patient has used cannabis, has it been affective?
- Has the patient experienced any unacceptable side effects?

Remember that if you didn't document it in the chart, you cannot prove it happened.

AN AFTERTHOUGHT: WORDS OF WARNING

Plant count is a unique part of cannabinoid medicine. While it has little or nothing to do with the clinical aspects of evaluating a patient it is an issue you need to be aware of for medical legal reasons. Some physicians charge an extra fee to authorize plant numbers in excess of six (6). An extra charge to approve a plant grow in excess of six (6) plants is, at best, highly ethically questionable. You should not charge an extra fee. In California any person who has a medical recommendation is entitled to grow as many plants as needed for their medical needs. In addition, plant count and flowering tops yields have only a passing similarity to each other.

Note: for more about plant count and yields, please see Appendix A.

CHAPTER 19
WHAT ABOUT THE FUTURE?

What's next?

- Increased use of Tinctures: Epidiolex (cannabidiol), dominant Sativex (nabiximols). These are two tinctures of cannabis pharmaceutical products.
- Off label use of synthetic △-9-THC: Marinol (dronabinol)
- Varieties/Strains: extracts vs. synthetics and/or single cannabinoids
- More research regarding Cannabinoids (CBG, CBC, CBD, phenoids, terpenes, and other constituents)
- Pharmaceuticalization v. Individual Freedom to Grow as described by Lester Grinspoon, M.D.

Top Three Needs

State legislatures are recognizing the need for product standardization and professionalism in growing, dispensing and prescribing cannabis. Basically, they are reinventing pharmacy and plant brand medicine.

1.) RESCHEDULING CANNABIS

The largest barrier to research and acceptance by the mainstream is that cannabis is schedule I. Making cannabis at least a Schedule II drug would make research much easier. Note: Many activists support de-scheduling cannabis and treating it like the plant it is. This would take us back more to the historical role of plant medicine.

2.) STANDARDIZATION

The desire and need for standardization with cannabis and other herbal medicinal products is widely recognized and has been for decades. All cannabis products should be lab tested and clearly show the product contents and dosage on the label.

3.) PROFESSIONALISM

- *Pharmacists*
  Cannabis was in the USP from 1850-1942 and was dispensed in pharmacies. That is who ought to be dispensing it.
- *Physicians*
  Medical schools need to teach about the ECS.
- *Practice Standards*
  The MD, ND, and/or NP needs to adhere to generally acceptable practice standards such as the Society of Cannabis Clinicians (SCC) and American Academy of Cannabinoid Medicine (AACM) standards.
- *Medical Cannabis Dispensaries*
  Dispensaries need to be professional just as pharmacies are today. A dispensary should be managed by a person with real medical training such as a nurse or pharmacist. Some states require physician direction, but that is overkill. Many states are already regulating them. While they should be treated like pharmacies, so far they are not. An option being looked at by some entrepreneurs is involving cannabis in a wholistic health spa model that incorporates a variety of physical and mental health treatment. With the advent of legalization laws, there are few medical-only dispensaries left. Some state laws prevent budtenders from talking about medical effects in any way.

  Sadly, there are few physicians in state legislation that often prioritizes the importance of tax revenue above all else. Dispensaries also are increasingly prioritizing recreational customers rather than offering more patient oriented services.

Research

The American Medical Association House of Delegates recognized that rescheduling would remove the barrier to research and clinical application. More research needs to be done on dose THC:CBD ratios, role of minor cannabinoids, terpenes, and especially cannabis for treating cancer and PTSD. At the time of this writing a human breast cancer trial in San Francisco was seeking funding. Dr. Sue Sisley was doing a PTSD study in Colorado and Arizona. Dr. Sisely has overcome numerous roadblocks, such as the Arizona State Senate cutting off funding for her position and the federal government providing moldy cannabis for human tests.

Areas to Focus on

- **Research**
  - o Standardization
  - o Plant Genomes
  - o Therapeutic role of terpenes, disease specific dosing, better understanding of the ECS
- **Laboratory**
  - o Labeling of products
  - o Product testing for:
    - Constituents, mold, pesticides, fertilizer
    - Terpene identification
    - Cannabinoid identification
    - *Note: Not all labs are created equal and states are still having trouble navigating regulation at this time.*
- **Disease Specific Research**
  - o PTSD
  - o Cancer
  - o Epilepsy
  - o ADD/ADHD
  - o Anxiety

- **Education**
  - o Medical: cannabis, cannabinoids, and the ECS to Pharmacy, Nursing, and Medical School Curriculum
  - o The following also need to be educated on cannabis, cannabinoids and the ECS
    - a) CME for practicing Health Care Providers
    - b) General Public
    - c) Law Enforcement
    - d) Legislative Bodies

APPENDIX A
CANNABIS PLANTS

Plant Count Does Not Accurately Reflect Potential Yield

There is enormous variability in both medical need and horticultural skills of a cannabis using patient. A good rule of thumb to remember is that in some instances doctors may need to justify their recommendation in a court of law.

Patients, in my practice, have grown plants that have resulted in everything from dead plants that produce nothing to 11 pounds of flowering tops on one plant grown by a landscaper.

There is no scientific basis for the use of a plant count to determine what number of plants will be needed to produce the dosage required to meet the patient's medical need. However, most cannabis cultivation regulations are based on plant count, despite the scientific incongruities.

The yield depends on many variables including but not limited to growers' interests and abilities, the plant's DNA, whether the cannabis medicine garden is outdoors or inside, type of lamps, horticultural skills, good luck, the weather, lack of pests, air, soil, light and fertilizer.

Chris Conrad is the author of *Yields and Dosages* and *Hemp Lifeline to the Future*. In *Yields and Dosages*, he explains how different variables can lead to similar yields. He also states, "most patients have difficulty gauging their future yield."

"Some harvests are better or worse for each grower. Some growers get better yields than others, but most fall in the middle, so using the average is the most reasonable basis to make projections. Outdoor plants typically yield more cannabis per plant than an indoor grow. Indoor plants each yield less but allow multiple harvests. Either way, it takes about 200 square feet of garden canopy to obtain six pounds of bud per year."[140]

Canopy is an agricultural term used to describe the area of the foliage of growing plants. The area shaded by foliage is called the canopy cover. The federal field data show that, on average, each square foot of mature, female outdoor canopy yields less than a half-ounce of dried and manicured bud. Conrad states that this is "consistent with growers' reports and gardens that have been seized by police as evidence and I have later weighed and examined."

He goes on, "All other things being equal, a large garden will always yield more than a small one, no matter how many plants it contains. This is true for skilled and unskilled gardeners alike. Restricting canopy will therefore limit any garden's total bud yield, no matter which growing technique is used or how many plants make up the combined canopy cover. Most patients can meet their medical need with 100 square feet of garden canopy."[141]

How Many Plants Is Too Many?

Conrad then goes on to discuss: How many are too many? He states, "it depends, since a few large cannabis plants can out-produce hundreds of small ones, the number of plants in a garden cannot accurately predict yield."[142]

In the Kelly decision, the California Supreme Court laid out a very practical plant standard, to wit a patient may grow as much cannabis as is required to meet the patient's medical needs.[143] This practical standard should be applied in your thinking on plant numbers if you make any plant recommendations. What you might consider is the patients usual plant yield. Also whether or not it is an indoor or outdoor grow may influence the yield.

[140] Conrad, Chris. *Cannabis Yields and Dosage: A Guide to the Production and Use of Medical Marijuana. Safe Access Now,* 2004. http://safeaccessnow.net/yieldsdosage.htm/.
[141] Ibid.
[142] Ibid.
[143] People v. Kelly (Patrick K.). 47 CAL. 4th 1008, 222 P.3D 186, 103 CAL. RPTR. 3D 733 (2010). https://www.leagle.com/decision/incaco20100121064/.

Having a hard and fast plant number, makes no sense since some plants produce as little as a quarter ounce of flowering tops and other plants may produce up to ten pounds of flowering tops. Any legislative body that uses plant numbers and not canopy area is ignoring good horticultural science. If you approve plant numbers just use reasonable assumptions on yield and medical need.

Conrad then goes on to discuss: How many are too many? He states, "it depends, since a few large cannabis plants can out-produce hundreds of small ones, the number of plants in a garden cannot accurately predict yield."[144]

In the Kelly decision, the California Supreme Court laid out a very practical plant standard, to wit: a patient may grow as much cannabis as is required to meet the patient's medical needs.[145] This practical standard should be applied here. By having a hard and fast plant number, regulations are ignoring good horticultural science.

---

[144] Conrad. Op. cit.
[144] People v. Kelly (Patrick K.). Op. cit.

APPENDIX B
RESOURCES ON CANNABINOIDS

More specific information regarding the state of the science investigating the beneficence of cannabinoids can be discovered from a variety of sources. The reader can find evidence on the subjects of successful treatment of pain, alcohol abuse, anxiety, depression, psychosis, the anti-inflammatory effects of cannabinoids, for treatment of autoimmune disorders, neurodegenerative disease, movement disorders, stroke and cancer.

- Breuer, A., Haj, C., Fogaca, M. et al. Fluorinated cannabidiol derivatives: enhancement of activity in mice models predictive of anxiolytic, antidepressant and antipsychotic effects. *PLoS One*. 2016:11 https://www.ncbi.nlm.nih.gov/pmc/articles/PMC 4945002/.
- Ceccarini, J., Hompes, T., Verhaeghen, A., et al. Changes in cerebral CB1 receptor availability after acute and chronic alcohol abuse and monitored abstinence. *Journal of Neuroscience*. 2014:34(8) 2822-2831.
- Gui, H., Liu, X., Wang, Z.W., He, D.Y., Su, D.F., Dai, S.M. Expression of cannabinoid receptor 2 and its inhibitory effects on synovial fibroblasts in rheumatoid arthritis. *Rheumatology* (Oxford). 2014:53(5) 802-809.
- Haj CG. Sumariwalla PF. Hanus L. et al. HU-444, a novel, potent anti-inflammatory, nonpsychotropic

cannabinoid. *Journal of Pharmacolology Experimental Therapy.* 2015:355(1) 66-75.

- Horvath, B., Magid, L., Mukhopadhyay, P. et al. A new cannabinoid CB2 receptor agonist HU-910 attenuates oxidative stress, inflammation and cell death associated with hepatic ischaemia/reperfusion injury. *British Journal of Pharmacology.* 2012:165(8) 2462-2478.

- Horvath, B., Mukhopadhyay P., Hasko G., Pacher P. The endocannabinoid system and plant derived cannabinoids in diabetes and diabetic complications. *American Journal of Pathology.* 2012:180(2) 432-442.

- Martin-Moreno, A.M., Reigada, D., Ramirez, B., et al. Cannabidiol and other cannabinoids reduce microglial activation in vitro and in vivo: relevance to Alzheimer's disease. *Mol Pharmacology.* 2011, 79(6) 964-973.

- Silveira, J.W., Issy, A.C., Castania, V.A. et al. Protective effects of cannabidiol on lesion-induced intervertebral disc degeneration. *PLoS One*, 2014:9(12) e 113161.

GLOSSARY
CANNABIS LEXICON*
David Bearman, M.D.

A

2-Arachidonoyl Glycerol (2AG): An endogenous ligand endocannabinoid of CB1 receptor.

Alcohol extraction: Cannabinoids are soluble in alcohol, both ethyl and isopropyl. Isopropyl is not safe to drink. Alcohol should be used as a solvent to remove alcohol soluble cannabinoids and essential oils from the trichomes.

Allosteric Binding: Partially into a receptor as with CBD into CB1 receptors.

Anandamid: One of the bodies' two endocannabinoids made from phosphatloyl: ethanolamine

B

Bhang: A traditional Indian tea made with cannabis leaves and/or roots.

Bidi: A small clay pipe used to smoke ganga.

Bong (Water Pipe): A device for smoking cannabis and filtering the smoke through water to remove irritants and cool the smoke. Water pipes deliver an inhalant that is cooler than from a cannabis cigarette (joint) and has 70% fewer irritants.

Butane Extraction: Butane is a solvent that may be used to extract butane-soluble constituents from cannabis flowering tops. This method is illegal in California because of the flammability dangers of butane.

C

Cannabidiol (CBD): One of over 100 cannabinoids found in cannabis. Cannabidiol is generally considered the second-most common cannabinoid in the plant. CBD has shown benefit for many conditions including autism, epilepsy, anxiety and cancer. It is psychoactive but is a non-euphoriant. CBD acts as an antagonist to THC, reducing its euphorogenic effects through allosteric binding.

Cannabis/Hemp: Per the late Richard Schultes, Ph.D., Harvard Professor and a pioneer entheogen expert, the distinction of .3% or less THC as hemp and .3% THC or more as cannabis is an arbitrary bureaucratic line. It is not based on botany or science. Hemp and cannabis are the same plant with one having more THC. Traditionally, hemp varieties have varying amounts of CBD but almost no THC.

Cannabinoid: Cannabinoids are 21 carbon molecules that block or stimulate CB1 and/or CB2 receptors. **(These include: CBC, CBCV, CBD, CBDA, CBDV, CBG, CBGV, CBN, CBV, THC, THCA, THCV.)**

—Phytocannabinoids are those cannabinoids (about 113) found within the cannabis plant.

—Endocannabinoids are cannabis like molecules produced by the human body. They are 2AG and anandamide.

—Both phytocannabinoids and endocannabinoids act upon the body's endocannabinoid receptors.

Cannabinoid (Acid Form): Raw or freshly harvested cannabis contains cannabinoids in the acid form. That is they have a carboxyl group. In the acid form (THCA, CBDA, etc.), the cannabinoids are not euphorogenic. They still carry various medicinal properties when consumed.

CB1/CB2: These are the two (2) principle human cannabinoid receptors. CB1 receptors are found largely in the brain and CB2 are largely in the immune system.

Charas: A term originally used in India to describe the resin from the plant. This is similar to hash but may also include buds and leaves.

Clone: A clipping from a cannabis plant, which can then be rooted and grown. Like many plants, cannabis can be asexually propagated via cloning. This creates a genetic copy of the "mother plant."

Closed-loop extraction: Chemical extraction (whether using a hydrocarbon solvent or CO_2) using a closed system. This means that the machine recycles the solvent rather than dispersing it in the air. Most commonly this is referring to a butane or propane extraction, but technically CO_2 extraction machines are also closed-loop.

CO_2 extraction: When high pressure is applied to CO_2, it becomes a liquid that is capable of working as a solvent that dissolves cannabinoids and essential oils from plant material. This process is a common method of making hash oil.

Concentrate: The word "concentrate" is very vague, as is the term "hash". Hash once referred only to the plant resin. Now any concentrated cannabis (e.g., water hash, pressed hash, wax, shatter, dry sieve (kief), pressed cannabis) may be referred to as hash.

It also refers to various cannabis tinctures in solution. These may be referred to as hash oils (BHO, CO_2 oil, shatter, wax, RSO, hemp oil, cannabis oil, milagro oil, etc.). These products are a concentrated form of cannabis. The THC level can be as high as 75-90%.

D

Dab (aka wax, shatter): This is a thick waxy concentrate that is consumed by placing it on a metal surface and heating that surface. The vapors are inhaled via a glass straw. The cannabinoids rapidly enter the blood through the alveoli walls. This leads to a rapid change in blood THC level.

Decarboxylate: Heat is required to remove the carboxyl group (decarboxylate) found in raw cannabis.

Dopamine: A neurotransmitter that affects intra- and extra-neural cell electrolyte concentrations. Dopamine helps depolarize the presynaptic neuron.

Dopamine Transporter: A neurotransmitter that binds free dopamine. It is thought by some researchers to be elevated in those with PTSD.

Drug: Emotionally laden or perjorative terms are often used in discussing drugs of abuse. This is true even down to how we define drugs. Some might say, "a drug is what a dope fiend uses." Other more medically oriented would say a drug is what is used to treat a diseas. This could include water, which is used for treating dehydration in infants, or sugar, used for treating insulin overdose, as drugs.

I prefer an even broader definition that a drug is any chemical which causes a physiological change in the bdoy. In other words, just about anything that can be ingested can be construed at some time as a drug.

Webster's *Third Collegiate Dictonary* defines a drug as "any substance used as a medicine or as an ingredient in a medicine." This definition shows how bias creeps into our thinking, in "a narcotic, hallucinogen," etc., especially one that is habit forming.

A more concise definition that I would substitute is, "A chemical substance, sometimes including food, which alters the normal state of the mind or body, or is used in the diagnosis or treatment of a disease."

Drug Abuse: The deliberate, non-therapeutic use of a drug, which if measured by dose, frequency, or route of administration proves to be detrimental to the individual either psychologically or physically. Pattern of drug use which chronically interferes with physical, psychological, social, or vocational functioning of the individual.

E

Edibles: Any cannabis product which is consumed orally and digested is considered an edible. There are many oral products including cannabis spiked soda, tea, tinctures, capsules, candy bars and gummy bears.

Endocannabinoid: System (ECS) All mammals have an ECS. It is essential for homeostasis. It consists, at a minimum, of two neurotransmitters anandamide and 2 AG, two receptors CB1 and CB2, and two enzymes FAAH and MAGL.

Endorphins: Endorphins are neurotransmitters which have been referred to as the body's self-produced opiates.

Entourage Effect (aka Ensemble Effect): The totality of the effect of all the therapeutic constituents of the plant acting in concert. Postulated in 1999 by Raphael Mechoulam, PhD.

Extract: See Concentrate.

F

FAAH: Fatty Acid Anhydrase. The enzyme that metabolizes anandamide.

Flower: Lay term for the female plant's racemes (horticulture term for flowers). See also Trichome.

Flowering Stage: Every cannabis plant goes through two distinct cycles in its lifetime: vegetative stage, when the plant is actively growing; and flowering stage, when the plant is focusing most of its energy on producing flowers.

G

Ganj/Ganja/Ghanja: In India cannabis is categorized as Bhang, Ganja or Charas. Ganga - the resin and leaves usually smoked in a clay pipe called a bide.

Germination: The initial growth phase of a cannabis plant's life, when it is grown from seed.

H

Hash, Hashish: Traditionally "hashish" refers to any collection of the resin glands (trichomes) of the cannabis plant. Collection of the trichomes is performed via a variety of methods (dry sieve, water extraction).

Hash oil, Honey Oil, FECO (fully extracted cannabis oil), Dabs, Rick Simpson Oil, RSO, Milagro Oil, Cannabis Oil, and Tincture: These are very non-specific term for cannabis in concentrated form.

Hookah: A smoking device that originated in India. It has a large centralized bowl and multiple hoses used to inhale the lighted contents of the bowl.

Hydroponics: A soil-less grow medium that delivers nutrients through water as opposed to dirt.

I

Indica: One of three varieties of cannabis along with sativa and ruderalis low in THC and higher in CBD and CBN. Recent lab studies have demonstrated that most strain names including sativa and indica are inconsistent and/or are inaccurate. They are largely marketing tools.

A more precise way to understand what is in a cannabis product is to read the label for the concentration of specific cannabinoids and terpenes.

These classifications are still used in the culture to help describe the differences between plants while they are growing. Indica varieties are sturdy shorter plants which mature more quickly. Indica varieties have been used for relieving pain, muscle tension, insomnia, anxiety, lack of appetite, reducing inflammation, and can have sedative effect.

J

Joint (see also: cone, spliff, doobie, reefer, mary jane, number): Cannabis rolled in cigarette rolling papers.

K

Kief: Kief is the traditional term for cannabis in Morocco.

L

Limbic System: The limbic system is one of the oldest parts of the human brain. It provides communication between the cerebral cortex, the newest more rational part of the brain and the midbrain or reptilian brain, the oldest part of the brain.

M

MAGL: monoacylglycerol lipase. The enzyme that metabolizes 2 AG.

Mary Jane: One of the numerous slang terms for cannabis. It is a play on "marijuana." Was once a somewhat discreet way of talking about cannabis. As cannabis enters the mainstream these slang and code names are declining in use.

Medicated: Term that medical cannabis consumers use to recognize that they are receiving cannabis' therapeutic value. Some say that they are medicated to indicate that they recently used cannabis.

Molecule Biochemical Configuration: Every molecule is a three dimensional object like a tinker toy model and parts of the molecule carry an electrical charge. This is its biological configuration. A molecule need not fit the receptor site like a glove. It is attracted by a relatively complementary shape and complementary charged receptor.

Because psychoactive substances have different biochemical configurations they only work on specific receptor sites within the brain. This is with the notable exception of alcohol. Alcohol is a non-specific neurodepressant. Its effects are not limited to any specific receptor sites.

Muggles: Popular 1920's name for cannabis, particularly by jazz musicians.

N

Neuron: A specialized nerve cell whose function is to carry electrical impulses from one end of the neuron to the other. It is composed of three parts: Axon, Dendrite and Cell Body. A neuron has two processes, axon and dendrite. The processes are branched, and transmit messages via electrical charges to and from the cell body.

—Axon: The discharging process; carries impulse away from the cell body.

—Dendrite: the receptive process; transmits impulse toward cell body.

—Synapse: the place where a nerve impulse is transmitted from one nerve to another.

The process that carries the electrical impulse toward the cell body is the dendrite. The other process, the axon, carries the electrical impulse away from the cell body.

Neurotransmitters: Neurotransmitters can cross the synaptic cleft and connect to receptor sites located in the post-synaptic cell. We know that the post-synaptic neuron has endo-cannabinoids that can go backward across the synaptic cleft.

NIDA: U.S. National Institute of Drug Abuse.

O

Orthostatic Receptor Binding: A molecule fitting into a receptor like a hand in a glove for instance anandamide into a CB1 receptor.

P

Percolator: Commonly known as a "perc," a percolator is a part of the more complicated glass water pipes that adds an additional water chamber to the equation, helping to provide more cooling and diffusion, which makes the smoke smoother.

Phenotype: Phenotype means "genetic expression." Each cannabis strain has two parent plants: one male and one female. When the female is pollinated by the male and produces seeds, those seeds contain the genetic material of both parents and the resulting plants have only that genetic material with which to work.

Excusing genetic mutations, a hybrid of two stable strains would product three distinct phenotypes: phenotype A, which leans more towards the mother; phenotype B, which leans more towards the father and phenotype C, which is a blend of the two. Growers will then select their favorite choices from the phenotypes displayed, choosing plants based on a variety of qualities including: appearance, aroma, taste, effect, flowering time and stature.

R

Receptor Site: The receptor site is a part of the nervous system (NS). The effect that a substance has depends on the role of the receptor site and whether the drug stimulates or blocks the receptor site. Cannabinoids effect CB1 and CB2 receptors.

Recreational (Adult) Use: Use of cannabis for social purposes rather than for primary medical purposes. It allows dispensaries to sell cannabis to clients who do not have a medical recommendation. In adult use states, anyone who is 21 or older can purchase cannabis by simply showing their ID.

Reefer: Possibly a version of the Mexican Spanish "grifa" or heavy marijuana user. Reefer became popularized in the 1920's as a term for a cannabis cigarette. It's best known for the propaganda film "Reefer Madness."

Retrograde Inhibition: A neuromodulation mechanism of the endocannabinoid system whereby cannabinoids increase the amount of dopamine released. The dopamine causes the presynaptic neuron to depolarize by effecting the intra- and extracellular electrolytes.

Route of Administration: To have an effect, a drug cannabis must first enter the body. It can do so through a number of portals of entry - sublingual, oral, respiratory (smoking, vaping), topical and anal.

S

Sativa: Sativa is generally a high THC low CBD plant. One of three major varieties of cannabis along with Indica and Ruderalis. Sativas can treat depression and fatigue because they are euphorogenic; they can decrease intraocular pressure, are anti-nauseants, can treat ADD/ADHD, PTSD and help with sleep. Their effects can definitely vary from user to user.

Sensimilla: From the Spanish meaning "without seed". It refers to cannabis with moderate to high THC which has no seeds.

Set, Setting, Previous Experience: Effects of psychoactive substances on the brain depend not only on the structure of the molecule but also on the amount consumed at any one time (dose), the weight of the individual, the set (what the user expects), the setting, the previous experience of the individual with that substance, the length of time the person has used the substance, the amount of food in the stomach and the presence of any other substances.

Side Effect: An effect other than that for which the drug was intended or the effect other than that required for its therapeutic effect. All drugs have side effects and most have several.

Spliff: A combination of tobacco and marijuana rolled together, that can at times be a cone shape, more often used in Europe. It can add a nicotine buzz to the high, but many people who don't smoke find it off-putting.

Synaptic Cleft: The nervous system is composed of separate neurons that communicate with one another via neurotransmitters. neurotransmitters. The space between two neurons is called the synaptic cleft. This is the space where the axon of one neuron terminates or ends near the dendrite of another neuron.

Since these two cells do not actually touch, a very small space exists between the membrane of the axon (the pre-synaptic cell) and the membrane of the dendrite (the post-synaptic cell). This space is known as the synaptic cleft. It poses a problem, since in most cases the electrical impulse that travels down the neuron is unable to cross this cleft.

Synaptic Transmission: If no other mechanism existed the impulse arriving at the end of the axon would be stopped. The mechanism that allows one neuron to communicate with the next is known as chemical transmission or synaptic transmission, to distinguish it from the electrical transmission which occurs within the nerve cell.

T

Terpene: With over 20,000 in nature, terpenes are the most ubiquitous class of molecules in nature. These are aromatic and flavorful and are found not only in cannabis but in nearly every other plant on the planet. Terpenes are found in essential oils. They are volatile, and evaporate at fairly low temperatures.

Terpenes also have medical benefits in themselves, as evidenced by the aromatherapy industry. Some of those super aromatic plants that seem to get you higher than the bland ones do. Many terpenes such as myrcene, limonene, linalool and pinene actually have a therapeutic value.

THC: Tetrahydrocannabinol (THC) is one of the main cannabinoids, along with CBD, found in the cannabis plant and is responsible for the majority of the plant's euphorogenic properties. THC has medical benefits including analgesic properties, though perhaps its most defined quality is its tendency to increase appetite.

Tincture: A liquid extraction of cannabis, often made with alcohol, olive or coconut oil. Tinctures are often administered sublingually (under the tongue) to help with quick absorption. Glycerin tinctures are sweeter, with almost syrup-like texture, while alcohol tinctures may have some burn, since they're often made with high-proof alcohol like everclear.

Topicals: Topicals are external applications of tincture of cannabis that can be used to treat muscle spasm, pain or skin conditions such psoriasis. These can include lotions, creams, balms. They don't give you any kind of high. Their terpene profile can contribute to their analgesic and anti-inflammatory effects.

Trichome: The trichomes are crystalline structures which coat the plant's bract and leaf surfaces. They contain the highest cannabinoid content in the plant. The heads are what is broken off and collected in high-grade dry sieve and water hashes, while the entire trichome is dissolved in solvent-based extracts.

V

Vaporizer: A vaporizer heats a cannabis product (whether it be flowers, hash, or oil), but not enough to be combusting. The heat of the vaporizer is just enough so that the volatile cannabinoids vaporize and can then be inhaled. This method has about 70% less irritants than smoking and no carcinogens such as benzpirene but still provide the immediate relief of inhalation.

Vegetative stage: Part of the cannabis plant's life cycle where it is actively growing rather than producing flowers. When the plant receives 12 hours of light or greater, it will continue growing vegetatively indefinitely; when the light cycle reaches 12 hours or less, then the plant will begin flowering. During the vegetative stage, the plants prefer a more blue spectrum of light, commonly produced by fluorescent or metal halide (MH) bulbs, whereas flowering plants prefer the more reddish light produced by high-pressure sodium (HPS) lighting.

W

Water hash (also called: bubble hash, full melt, iceolator hash, ice wax, jermichael, melt, solventless wax): Water hash involves a set of microscreen extraction bags, ice, and water. It is a method to concentrate THC. Fresh frozen pant material is preferred to make the best final product, though dry material is also used regularly.

Wax: Wax is made from hash oil, generally after being whipped over heat in order to introduce air into the product. Wax can simply be crumbled on top of a bowl to add an extra punch.

* This Lexicon is based in part on a glossary by Ry Prichard and Jake Browne, in The Cannabist

About the Authors

David Bearman received his M.D. from the University of Washington School of Medicine. He has served at all levels of government including the U.S. Public Health Service, Director of Health Services at San Diego State University, Health Officer and Director Sutter County Health Department and Medical Director and Director of Medical  Services for the Santa Barbara Regional Health Authority (now CenCal). He is the author of *Drugs Are NOT The Devil's Tools.*

Dr. Bearman has a long and illustrative half-century career in the field of drug abuse treatment and prevention. He was prominent in the community clinic movement, having started the third Free Clinic in the country in Seattle, then directing the Haight Ashbury Drug Treatment Program, and in 1970 founding the Isla Vista Medical Clinic. He was Medical Director of Santa Barbara County Methadone Maintenance Clinic and Ventura County Opiate Detox Program, and Zona Seca, an outpatient drug treatment program.

He is a leader in the field of cannabinoid medicine and is a co-founder of the American Academy of Cannabinoid Medicine, past board member of Americans for Safe Access and the Advisory Board for Patients Out of Time. The Wall Street Journal Health Blog declared him their Doctor of the Day.

He has taught courses on the physiology and history of substance use and abuse at UCSF, UCSB, and SDSU, been a consultant to Hoffman LaRoche, NIDA and the National

PTA, made numerous professional presentations and consulted widely and has been an expert witness in over 400 civil, criminal, and family court cases. Currently he is Zona Seca's Medical Consultant, maintains a private practice, as well as frequently serving as an expert witness.

Dr. Bearman developed an early interest in medicine when working in his father's pharmacy in Rice Lake, Wisconsin as a high school and college student. He graduated from the University of Wisconsin in 1963 with a degree in Psychology and in 1967 obtained his M.D. degree from the University of Washington School of Medicine. He now maintains a private practice as a specialist in pain management and cannabinoid medicine in Goleta, California where lives with his wife, Lily (a career counselor). They have two adult children, Samantha and Benjamin.

Maria Pettinato, RN, PhD, is an Associate Professor in the College of Nursing at Seattle University, Seattle, Washington. She is an experienced faculty member teaching Patho-physiology, Neurobiology, and Med/Surg nursing in both under-graduate and graduate programs on the east and west coast of the United States for the past 25 years. Her research interests focus on sexual minority health issues and medicinal cannabis. Her scholarly work focuses on substance use, mental health issues, and sexual minority health issues.

She is the author of *Medicinal Cannabis: A Primer for Nurses.*

Index

A

Abrams, Donald, 51, 81
Adenosine Triphosphate (ATP), 19, 22, 74
ADHD (ADD), 15-18, 23, 39, 47-52, 64-65, 79, 93, 100, 102, 116, 132, 134, 137
Agurel, Stig, 104
Aizpurua-Olaizola, 26, 28
Alcohol extraction, 49, 55, 125
Allosteric Binding, 10, 14, 20, 24, 32, 125-126
Altmann, Karl-Heinz, 37
Alzheimer's disease, 29-30, 32, 66, 68, 124
American Academy of Cannab-inoid Medicine (AACM), 68, 71, 107, 115, 139
American Medical Association, 4, 7-8, 116, 124
American Medical Association (AMA), 4, 7-8
American Society of Addiction Medicine (ASAM), 78
Amygdala, 10
Analgesia, 13, 28, 48, 64, 67-68, 87
Analgesic Dose, 48
Anandamid, 125
Anandamide, 10-11, 15, 32, 67-68, 70, 126, 129, 132
Andyrsiak, Therese, 52
Angiogenic Growth Factor (AGF), 72, 84
Anti-Proliferative Dose, 49
Anxiety Relief Dose, 49
Apoptosis, 49, 64, 71-73, 84
Appointment Length, 110
Areas to Focus on
    Disease Specific Research, 116
    Education, 117
    Laboratory, 116
    Research, 116
Arnaud, Claire, 86
Asakura, Masanori, 85
Atrioventricular Septal Defects (AVSD), 85
Auréli, Marco, 70
Autism, 49, 51, 65, 126
Autoimmune Diseases, 36, 65

B

Baker, Laura A., 79, 86
Bearman, David, 71, 125, 139
Benowitz, Neal L., 97
Benson, John A., 67, 76, 94
Beta-Caryophyllene, 36, 39
Bhang, 54, 125, 129
Bidi, 125
Bigdeli, Mohammad Reza, 71
Bilateral Common Carotid Artery Occlusion (BCCAO), 70
Bin, Jianping, 85
Bipolar disorder, 15, 23, 65-66
Bisogno, Tiziana, 37
Blood Pressure (BP), 24, 79-80, 84, 97, 109
Blood THC Levels, 101-102, 104
Bong, 53, 60, 82, 125
Botany of Cannabis, 3
Brain Affected by Cannabinoids, 24
Brain Relieve Pain, 67
Breuer, A, 123
Browne, Jake, 137
Bruno, Patricia L., 33
Bureau of Narcotics and Dangerous Drugs (BNDD), 8
Burger, Fabienne, 86
Bush, George H.W., 9
Butane Extraction, 125
Butorac, Mario, 41

C

California Medical Cannabis Research Center (CMCR), 28, 76
Calignano, Antonio, 15
Calvarese, Barry, 82-83
Cancer, 12, 21, 27, 29-37, 44, 49-51, 56, 60, 64, 66, 71-75, 83-84, 87, 92, 116, 123, 126
Cancer Chemoprevention, 72

Cannabene Hydride, 27
Cannabichromene (CBC), 26, 30, 114, 126
Cannabidiol (CBD), 14-15, 19-22, 26, 28-33, 39, 44-59, 62, 67-72, 75, 81, 85, 87, 109, 114, 116, 123-126, 130, 134-135
Cannabigerol (CBG), 26, 28-30, 39, 49, 67, 114, 126
Cannabinoid (Acid Form), 126
Cannabinoid Common Effects, 15
Cannabinoids in Acid Form, 33
Cannabinol (CBN), 26, 28-31, 49, 62, 67, 126, 130
Cannabis
    Chemical Characteristics, 26
    Driving, 79-80, 101-104
    Half Life, 63
    IQ, 79, 86-87
    Mechanisms of Action, 73
    Metabolized, 62-63
    Receptors, 10-14
    Therapeutic Applications, 64
Cannabis Dependency, 94-95, 97, 100
Cannabis Needs
    Professionalism, 115
    Rescheduling Cannabis, 114
    Standardization, 114-115
Cannabis Plant, 3, 22, 26, 35, 37, 40-41, 46, 54, 59, 105, 119-121, 126-130, 135-136
Cannabis sativa, 3, 26, 28
Cannabis Time Line, 4
Canopy, 120-121
Cardiovascular Effects, 84-85
Castania, V.A, 124
CB1, 10, 14, 20, 24, 26, 29, 32-33, 50, 63, 73, 85, 123-126, 129, 132-133
CB2, 10, 14, 17, 26, 29, 32, 37, 73, 85-86, 124, 126, 129, 133
Ceccarini, J, 123
Characteristics of Cannabis, 26
Charas, 127, 129
Chen, Jian-Zhong, 37
Cichewicz, Diana, 71
Cimino, Nina M., 62

Clinical Standards, 107, 109, 111, 113
Clone, 127
Closed-loop extraction, 127
CO2 extraction, 127
Cobian, Eloy Pulido, 41
Concentrate, 67, 127, 129, 137
Conditions Cannabi, 64
Conrad, Chris, 119
Constituents of the Plant, 27-28, 49, 129
Coronary Artery Risk Development in Young Adults (CARDIA), 86
Courtney, William, 59
Crohn's Disease, 18, 33, 54, 65
Curran, Valerie, 87
CYP2C, 53
CYP3A, 53

D

Dab, 127, 130
Dai, S.M, 123
DEA Rescheduling Hearing, 9
Decarboxylate, 33, 128
Decarboxylation, 33, 59
Devitt-Lee, Adrian, 20
Diagnostic and Statistical Manual of Mental Disorders (DSM), 96, 98-99
Disorder Considerations, 100
Dopamine, 11, 15, 17-18, 128, 133
Dopamine Transporter, 11, 17, 128
Dosing, 40-41, 43, 45, 47, 49, 51, 58, 81, 87, 116
Dowd, Maureen, 81
Driving Under the Influence (DUI), 104
Dronabinol, 16, 32, 44, 47-48, 50-52, 54-58, 75, 96, 102, 105-106, 109, 114
    Side Effects, 44-50
Drug Abuse, 78, 100, 105, 128, 132, 139
Drug: Harm Reduction Substitute, 71
Dysphoria, 32-34, 39, 46-47, 49-51, 54, 57, 79-81, 87

E

Edibles, 54, 82, 129
Educational Discussion, 111
Educational Material, 110
Ellison, George W., 52
Endocannabinoid, 10-15, 21, 25, 32, 65, 68, 70-71, 97, 104, 110-112, 124-126, 129, 132-133
Endocannabinoid Deficiency Syndrome, 15, 23, 65, 73, 97, 105
Endocannabinoid Receptors, 11, 14, 126
Endocannabinoid System (ECS), 10-17, 21-25, 39, 68, 85, 104, 110-112, 115-117, 124, 129, 133
Endorphins, 67-68, 129
Ensemble Effect, 37, 129
Entourage Effect, 37-39, 44-45, 57, 129
Epidiolex, 44, 54-55, 114
Epilepsy, 4, 28, 32-33, 45, 51-52, 66, 116, 126
Etxebarria, Nestor, 26

F

Fairbanks, Lynn, 52
Fatty Acid Anhydrase (FAAH), 10-11, 32, 129
Flower, 3, 35-36, 40, 42, 129, 136
Flowering Stage, 129
Fogaca, M, 123
Fonseca, Fernando Rodriguez de, 15
Food and Drug Administration (FDA), 28, 44, 56, 58, 76, 83, 101-102
Fride, Ester, 37
Frossard, Jean-Louis, 86
Full Extracted Cannabis Oil (FECO), 49, 130
Funahashi, Tatsuya, 62

G

G-Coupled Protein Receptors (GCPR), 20
Gagliardi, Rubens, 52
Gamma-aminobutyric acid (GABA), 10, 36

Ganj, 129
Gastrointestinal, 12, 65
Germination, 129
Gertsch, Jürg, 37
Gillespie, Hamp, 104
Giuffrida, Andrea, 15
Gorriti, Miguel Angel, 15
Grammatikopoulo, Gerasimos, 15
Gray, Robert, 86
Grinspoon, Lester, 38, 114
Gui, H, 123
Guimarães, Francisco Silveira, 70
Guy, Geoffrey W., 32

H

Haj, C, 123
Hart, Carl L., 90
Hashish, 41, 94, 130
Hasko G, 124
Herning, Ronald I., 97
High-THC Cannabis, 32, 87
Hill, Dennis, 73
Hind, William H., 85
Hollister, Leo, 104
Homeostasis, 12-15, 25, 71-72, 129
Hompes, T, 123
Hookah, 130
Horvath, B, 124
Horwood, L. John, 91-92
Huang, Susan M., 68
Hudgins, Rebekah, 91
Hulley, Stephen Benjamin, 86
Human Brain
  midbrain, 23-24
  neocortex, 23
  reptilian brain, 23-24
Hydroponics, 130

I

Iacono, William G., 79, 86
Indica, 6, 45, 130, 134
Institute of Medicine (IOM), 5, 75-76, 80, 94
Intracellular Organelles, 19
Investigational New Drug (IND) Program, 5, 42
Irons, Daniel, 79, 86
Isen, Joshua D., 79, 86

Issy, A.C, 124

J

James, Deborah, 86
Joint, 41, 43, 82, 96, 125, 130
Jones, Reese, 96
Juicing, 33-34, 50, 54, 59

K

Karsak, Meliha, 37
Khoddam, Rubin, 79, 86
Kief, 127, 131
Kimura, Toshiyuki, 62
Kitakaze, Masafumi, 85

L

Lander, N., 52
Lawn, John, 9
Ledent, Catherine, 85
Lee, Martin, 14, 19
Leonti, Marco, 37
Limbic System, 23-24, 131
Limonene, 36, 39, 51, 73, 135
Linalool, 36, 39, 135
Liu, Kiang, 86
Liu, X, 123
Lodge, Jon W., 83
Luo, Tao, 85

M

Mach, François, 86
Magid, L, 124
MAGL, 11, 129, 131
Marcu, Jahan, 14
Marihuana Tax Act, 8
Marinol; see Dronabinol
Martin-Moreno A.M., 124
Mary Jane, 130-131
Marzo, Vincenzo Di, 37
Mathre, Mary Lynn, 42
McGue, Matt, 79, 86
Mechoulam, Raphael, 28, 37, 52, 129
Medical Board of California (MBC), 108
Medical Review Officers (MRO), 105-106
Medicated, 131

Melamede, Robert, 25
Mental Health, 65, 98, 115, 140
Metabolism, 50, 62-63
Methicillin-Resistant Staphylococcus
    Aureus (MRSA), 31, 39
Meyer, Erika, 70
Migraine, 4, 7, 16, 18, 23, 45, 60, 66, 112
Milani, Humberto, 70
Mild Withdrawal Symptoms, 96, 99
Mitochondria, 14, 19-22, 70, 72, 74
Mixing linalool and limonene, 39
Molecule Biochemical Configura-
    tion, 131
Monoterpenes, 35, 72-73
Monti, Andrea, 3
Morgan, John P., 91
Motor Control, 66
Muggles, 131
Mukhopadhyay, P, 124
Myers, Lawrence W., 52
Myrcene, 35, 39, 135

N

Nabiximols, 16, 44, 47-48, 52, 54-55, 57, 75, 114
National Highway Traffic Safety
    Administration's (NHTSA), 101-103
National Institute on Drug Abuse
    (NIDA), 78, 84, 89-91, 94-95, 132, 139
Navarro, Miguel, 15
Navarro, Patricia, 26
Neurodegeneration, 66
Neurodegenerative Disease, 29, 66, 68, 123
Neuron, 16-18, 69, 128, 132-135
Neuroprotective, 22, 30, 33, 67-68
Neurotransmitters, 10-11, 129, 132, 135
NIDA Study, 90
Non-cannabinoid receptors, 14
Non-Scientific Adult Dose, 46
Normal Adult Dosage of THC, 46
Northstone, Kate, 91-92
Nugent, Kevin, 91
Nung, Shen, 4, 6

O

Ohlsson, Agneta, 104
Oliveira, Rúbia Maria Weffort de, 70
Olsen, James L., 83
Oral Dose, 48, 81
Oral Ingestion, 54
Orthostatic Receptor Binding, 132

P

Pacher P, 124
Pain Relief, 3, 7, 48, 61, 68, 74, 76, 78
Patent Medicine, 45
Patient Evaluation, 108
Pelli, Graziano, 86
Percolator, 132
Pereira, Aparecido E., 52
Petrocellis, Luciano De, 37
Pettinato, Maria, 140
Phenotype, 133
Physical Exam, 108, 110, 112
Physician-Patient Relationship, 108
Phytol, 36
Pimentel, Camilo, 52
Pinene, 35-36, 38-39, 50, 135
Plant Potency, 40
Pletcher, Mark James, 86
Pollack, Sarah F., 33
Pollan, Michael, 3, 40
Positive Cardiovascular Effects, 85
Practice Pattern, 109
Pre-Visit Screening, 109
Prenatal Cannabis Exposure, 90, 92
Principle Endocannabinoid System
    Components, 11
Psychiatric diagnoses, 98
Psychomotor Impairment, 101
PTSD, 18, 23, 49, 64, 66-67, 79, 93,
    97, 100, 116, 128, 134
Pulgar, Teresa Gómez del, 68

R

Racz, Ildiko, 37
Raduner, Stefan, 37
Raine, Adrian, 79, 86
Ramaekers, Johannes Gerardus, 104
Ramirez, B, 124
Ramos, Oswaldo L., 52

Receptor Site, 73, 131-133
Record Keeping, 111
Recreational (Adult) Use, 133
Reefer, 81, 111, 130, 133
Reigada, D, 124
Reiss, Sheldon, 83
Residual Levels of THC, 104
Respiratory
    Smoking, 60
    Vaporizing, 60
    Water Pipe, 60
Respiratory Dose, 47
Retrograde Inhibition, 12, 15-17, 67,
    112, 133
Rhe, Man-Hee, 45
Route of Administration, 46, 50, 81,
    83, 88, 112, 128, 134
Russo, Ethan, 38, 42

S

Sadile, Adolfo G., 15
Sañudo-Peña, M. Clara, 68
Sanvito, W. L., 52
Sativa, 3, 26, 28, 130, 134
Sativex; see Nabiximols
Schibano, Daniele, 26
Schultes, Richard E, 3
Seizures, 17, 33, 51-52, 55-56, 58, 60,
    66
Sensimilla, 134
Shapiro, Bertrand J., 82-83
Sheskin, Tzviel, 37
Side Effect, 9, 32, 38, 58, 82, 134
Side Effects of Smoking
    Bronchospasm, 82
    Cough, 82
    Sputum Production, 82
Sidney, Stephen, 86
Silveira, J.W, 124
Simmons, Michael S., 82
Simsir, Yilmaz, 26
Sisley, Dr. Sue, 116
Sluis, Willem van der, 41
Smoking, 43, 47-48, 53, 60, 81-87, 93-
    96, 104, 125, 130, 134, 136
Soares, Ligia Mendes, 70
Sodium-Calcium Exchanger (NCX),
    14, 71
Spasticity, 31, 52

Sphingolipid Rheostat, 73-74
Spliff, 130, 134
Staub, Christian, 86
Strangman, Nicole M., 68
Stroke, 67-68, 70-71, 123
Symbiosis, 19
Synaptic Cleft, 132, 134-135
Synaptic Transmission, 135
synthetic cannabinoid, 68-69
Szara, Stephen, 94

T

Takashima, Seiji, 85
Takeda, Shuso, 62
Tamiri, Tsippy, 37
Tashkin, Donald P., 82, 84
Terpene, 3, 26-27, 35-39, 44, 46, 49-50, 53, 57-58, 67, 72, 74, 83, 105, 109-110, 114, 116, 130, 135-136
Tetrahydrocannabinol (THC), 3, 10, 12, 14-15, 21-22, 26, 28-33, 36-63, 67, 71-75, 80-83, 86-87, 90, 96, 99-106, 109, 114, 116, 126-127, 130, 134-137
Tetrahydrocannabivarin (THCV), 31, 106, 126
Therapeutic Dose, 46
Thiele, Elizabeth A., 33
Tincture, 5, 45, 48, 53-55, 61, 82, 114, 127-130, 136
Topicals, 136
Torres, Ciara A., 89
Tourette's Syndrome, 15, 65-66
Toxicology, 63, 105-106
Traumatic Brain Injury (TBI), 67-69, 79, 93
Treating Cancer, 49, 116
Trichome, 125, 129-130, 136
Tsou, Kang, 68
Tuvblad, Catherine, 79, 86
Two Arachidonoyl Glycerol (2AG), 10, 125-126

U

U.S. Department of Transportation (DOT), 101, 103, 106
Ulrich-Merzenich, G., 38

Ungerleider, Thomas, 52
Unhigh, 87
United States Pharmacopeia (USP), 7, 115
University of California at Irvine (UCI), 15
University of California at San Diego (UCSD), 5, 28, 76
University of California at San Francisco (UCSF), 51, 76, 81, 95, 139
University of New Mexico, 77
Urine Testing, 105
Usobiaga, Aresatz, 26

V

Vaporization, 48, 60, 82
Vaporizer, 60, 136
Vegetative stage, 129, 136
Veillard, Niels R., 86
Venturi, Gianpietro, 3
Verhaeghen, A, 123

W

Wang, Z, 123
Water hash, 127, 136-137
Watkinson, Barbara, 86
Wax, 127, 137

X

Xie, Xiang-Qun, 37
Xu, Dingli, 85

Y

Yamamoto, Ikuo, 62
Yamaori, Satoshi, 62

Z

Zhao, Hui, 85
Zimmer, Andreas, 37, 86
Zimmer, Lynn, 91
-

Understanding history is a great step doctors can take when educating themselves about the stigmas and realities associated with cannabis.

DRUGS ARE NOT THE DEVIL'S TOOLS

The History of Drugs:
Discrimination, Greed, the War on Drugs and
Why Medical Marijuana is Creating a New Paradigm

David Bearman, M.D.

Foreword by Judge James Gray

2637 B.C.E. to Present

Revised One Volume Color Edition

Drugs are NOT the Devil's Tools is an engaging, thoughtful, beautifully illustrated and well-researched examination into the origin of United States drug laws and a prescription for change, a new paradigm.

Dr. David Bearman shows how, through intertwining motives of discrimination and greed, often under the guise of morality, the government has created a drug policy that is completely dysfunctional. As he points out, our drug laws have been very effective in further marginalizing already discriminated-against groups and a total failure in every other respect.

In this entertaining and informative book, Dr. Bearman shows that there has rarely been a civilization in the history of mankind that has not used some form of mind-altering substance. He also demonstrates that the very real medical properties of cannabis were recognized thousands of years ago and are being further explored today, hampered only by the absurd U.S. drug policy.

Full Color Edition: $65 • Black & White Edition: $45

For more information and to learn more go to:

www.drugsarenotthedevilstools.com

Available on Amazon

For quantity orders, contact Dr. David Bearman's Medical Practice, 805-961-9988

Order Form

To order copies of *Drugs Are NOT The Devil's Tools* in color or black & white or *Cannabis Medicine,* fill out this form and:

- **Fax it to: 805-961-9966**
- **Scan it in and email it to: dbearman420@gmail.com**
- **Mail it to:**

> **Dr. David Bearman's Medical Practice**
> **7394 Calle Real, Suite C**
> **Goleta, CA 93117**

For quantity orders please email dbearman420@gmail.com

# of Bks	Title	Price	Total
	Drugs Are NOT The Devil's Tools (Color edition)	$65.00	
	Drugs Are NOT The Devil's Tools (B&W edition)	$45.00	
	Cannabis Medicine	**$25.00**	
	Shipping: $4.00-first book, $2.00 @ additional		
		TOTAL DUE:	

Name on card:_____ Date:_____

CC#:_____ Exp.Date:_____

Billing Address:_____

Billimg Zip:_____ Security Code on back of Card:_____

Ship To Address:_____ Zip:_____

Phone:_____ Email:_____

To pay by check: Make payable to Dr. David Bearman's Medical Practice

7394 Calle Real, Suite C Goleta, CA 93117 · 805-961-9988

King Harvest
(2x pm) @ hs for sleep
(synergy) 7-10 gtts in capsule

KAVYA
Dr Mary Sebastian
Gastroenterologist

fax: 404 778 4560
        ph: 3184
send: name ε DOB
        ID + Ins.

appt 9/21 @ 2:45
✗ Emory Clinic Gastroenterology
1365 Clifton Road Clinic
Building B (across
        from E. Un. Hosp.)
8³⁰-5pm
8ᴬᴹ

---

www.Emoryhealthcare.org
404 727 8820   patient
                portal

Made in the USA
Columbia, SC
02 August 2020

15318210R00088